To Beverley

with all my love

**PATHFINDER
COMPANY**

G. Gill

PATHFINDER COMPANY
44 PARACHUTE BRIGADE
The Philistines

Graham Gillmore

30° South Publishers

Graham Gillmore enjoys country life in the natural beauty of East Anglia and the Fens but was born a Londoner in 1952. An innate fascination with history and all things military inevitably led him to joining the Grenadier Guards, and for six months the Guards Depot drilled into him soldiering skills of the highest standard. Graham left the British Army in 1977 to join the Rhodesian Light Infantry in their war to prevent Communist guerrillas overthrowing the country. After two years as the signals rep to Support Commando, 1RLI, Graham was promoted to Signals Troop Sergeant. With the fall of Rhodesia to the Marxists in 1980, he moved to South Africa to continue the anti-terrorist fight with the Pathfinder Company, 44 Parachute Brigade. He returned to England still on crutches after being wounded in Angola and joined the Territorial Army. After a career in VIP security Graham is now a leading member of the Victorian Military Society for whom he runs The Diehard Company, an internationally renowned re-enactment group. He advises and writes articles on the British Army on Home Service and on campaign during Queen Victoria's reign.

Published in 2010 by 30° South Publishers (Pty) Ltd.

3 Ajax Place, 120 Caroline Street, Brixton

Johannesburg 2092, South Africa

www.30degreessouth.co.za

info@30degreessouth.co.za

Copyright © Graham Gillmore, 2010

Design and origination by 30° South Publishers (Pty) Ltd.

Printed and bound by Pinetown Printers, Durban

ISBN 978-1920143-48-0

For years after returning to England from Africa I would talk to ex-servicemen and they would say, "Oh yes, Rhodesia, I was going to go there". I replied that while we were similar the difference was that I got on the plane and they didn't. So this book is dedicated to all those others who made that decision to get on the plane, to those who answered the call to duty and to put their lives at risk in order to protect the innocent from the evils of communist-inspired terrorism.

It is also dedicated to the memory of those pathfinders who are no longer with us but have blazed a trail toward that last great mystery:

Steven Hadlow, Great Britain
Bob Beech, Rhodesia
John Wessels, Rhodesia
Art Nulty, Great Britain
Chris Rogers, New Zealand
Terry Tangney, Australia
Bruce Firkin, Great Britain

These men, like the others, lived a life of perilous adventure, the spirit of which is possibly summed up by a long-remembered quote:

Colonel Breytenbach taking questions after an op briefing:
Pathfinder: "What time does the operation begin?"
Colonel: "What time does the bar close?"

This book consists wholly of the written and photographic contributions of ex-members of the Pathfinder Company without whose encouragement and assistance this book could not have been possible. What started as an idea by Rich Malson grew into this history of a unique unit. In particular, the support of the following people is gratefully acknowledged:

Colonel Jan Breytenbach VRD, SD, SM, MMM
Dr Alastair MacKenzie PhD MSc, Lt-Col (Rtd)
Dave Barr
Gordon Brindley
Jim Burgess
Dennis Croukamp BCR
Dean Evans
Nelson Fishbach
Ken Gaudet
Rob Gilmour
Rich Malson
Peter McAleese
Peter Morpuss
Lang Price
Sean Wyatt

CONTENTS

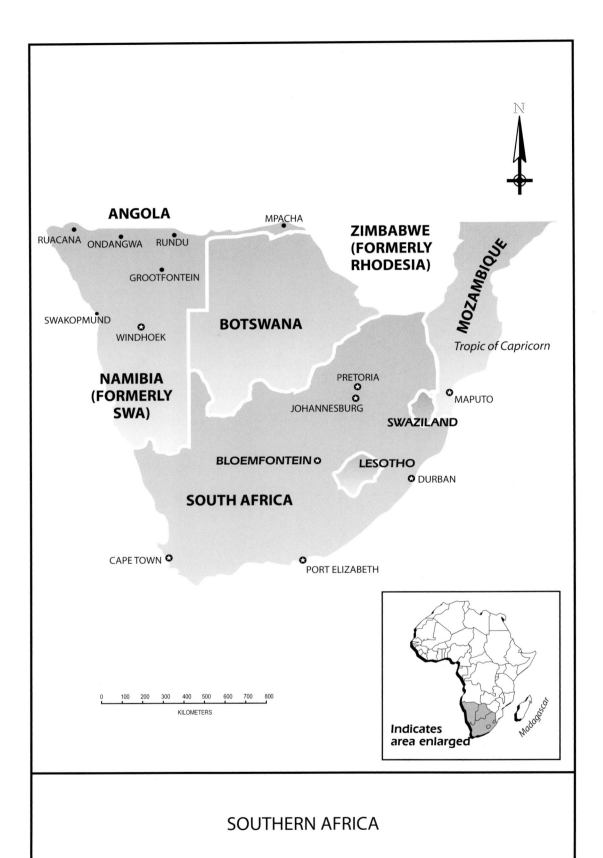

ANGOLA

MPACHA

RUACANA ONDANGWA RUNDU

ZIMBABWE
(FORMERLY
RHODESIA)

GROOTFONTEIN

MOZAMBIQUE

SWAKOPMUND

BOTSWANA

WINDHOEK

Tropic of Capricorn

NAMIBIA
(FORMERLY
SWA)

PRETORIA

MAPUTO

JOHANNESBURG

SWAZILAND

BLOEMFONTEIN

LESOTHO

DURBAN

SOUTH AFRICA

CAPE TOWN

PORT ELIZABETH

0 100 200 300 400 500 600 700 800

KILOMETERS

Madagascar

Indicates
area enlarged

SOUTHERN AFRICA

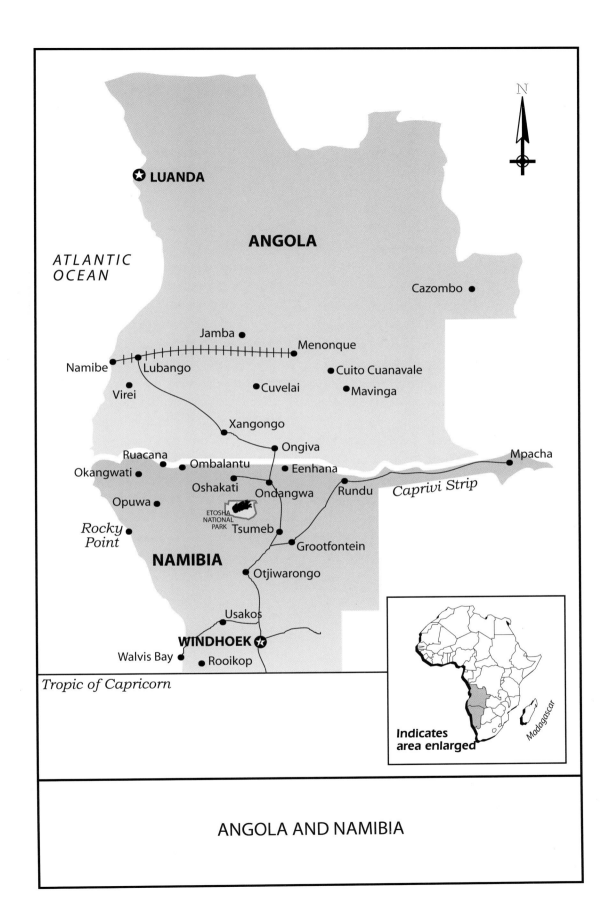

N

LUANDA

ANGOLA

ATLANTIC
OCEAN

Cazombo ●

Jamba ●
Menonque ●
Namibe Lubango
Cuito Cuanavale ●
Virei ● Cuvelai ●
Mavinga ●

Xangongo ●
Ongiva ●
Ruacana ● Mpacha ●
Okangwati ● Ombalantu ● Eenhana ●
Oshakati ● Ondangwa ● Rundu ● *Caprivi Strip*
Opuwa ●
ETOSHA
NATIONAL
PARK Tsumeb ●
*Rocky
Point* ● Grootfontein ●
NAMIBIA Otjiwarongo ●

Usakos ●
WINDHOEK ☆
Walvis Bay ● Rooikop ●

Tropic of Capricorn

**Indicates
area enlarged** *Madagascar*

ANGOLA AND NAMIBIA

Foreword

On Ascension Day, 1978, a composite South African parachute battalion jumped onto the tactical HQ of SWAPO's PLAN army, based at Cassinga, 250 kilometres north of the Angolan-South West African (now Namibian) border to destroy the facility, their logistics, and to wipe out a strong concentration of SWAPO guerrillas that had gathered in preparation for a massive incursion into South West Africa (SWA) via forward operational bases to disrupt the first democratic elections scheduled for SWA later that year.

The airborne assault, part of Operation Reindeer, was an unqualified success because the whole base was destroyed, never to be used again. Six hundred and eight PLAN fighters were killed, with many more wounded, which pushed the final SWAPO death toll to well above a thousand. We only lost four paratroopers killed in action plus a dozen or so wounded.

According to airborne experts from elsewhere, especially in Britain and Australia, this was the most audacious parachute assault executed since the Second World War, keeping in mind that the mounting airfield was well over a thousand nautical miles away to the southeast. I was the commander of that airborne assault which, although successful above all expectations, also highlighted many shortcomings, some of which almost led to a disastrous outcome to the battle.

When I was tasked to form 44 Parachute Brigade later that year, I resolved that what was needed as a first priority was a pathfinder company that could overcome the drawbacks I had encountered. Such a company was nothing new of course. During the Second World War the first mass parachute drops were accompanied by excessive confusion and loss in lives as paratroopers were scattered all over the countryside, rarely close to or on top of their targets. This necessitated the formation of a specially trained and manned organization that could be dropped ahead of the main airborne assault to guide aircraft to the correct drop zones and to assist paratroopers to quickly concentrate into their tactical organizations and

formations in order to fully exploit the surprise factor always associated with airborne assaults. Thus, towards the end of World War Two, airborne assaults became ever more successful mainly because parachute drops were no longer going disastrously astray.

I pinpointed a few areas of real concern after the Reindeer operation. The most important problem was the fact that the DZs selected from a wrongly scaled air photo were too short for 32-man sticks dropped from the C-130s and C-160s, and that the drops therefore were way off target. The depth of the somewhat insignificant-looking river could not be gauged from the air photos, thus one man was drowned and the mortar platoon lost half its equipment when weapon containers had to be dumped in the river to prevent drowning of personnel. The presence of anti-aircraft guns was not detected because the air photos were out of date. Because the drop went astray the concentration and forming up into attack formation took far too long so that the shock effect of the preliminary bombing runs had worn off by the time the assault was launched by the two assault companies. The rest of the companies, deploying into cut-off positions, took too much time doing so with the result that too many SWAPOs managed to escape the net, including Dimo Amaambo, the commanding general of PLAN. The extraction of the paratroopers by helicopter was also somewhat chaotic. More negative results were, of course, added by me on subsequent reflection.

I, therefore, visualized that all future airborne assaults be preceded by the deployment of pathfinder teams to overcome all the disadvantages mentioned above. In addition, I wanted teams on the ground, virtually on a permanent basis and right inside the guerrilla base area, to locate juicy targets for airborne assaults. Thus the pathfinders had to be proficient in many 'specialities' not common to even elite paratroopers. The list is almost endless.

I firstly wanted to rely on my own deep-reconnaissance capability in order to 'find the enemy' and then to have the subsequent airborne assault executed with nothing less than one-hundred-percent effectiveness. These demands required highly specialized teamwork from small pathfinder teams with all the skills necessary to make them effective, such as navigation (this was before GPS of course), bush craft and survival, signals, weapons training, tracking and counter-tracking, escape and evasion techniques, a high level of field medical capacity, small-team tactics, OP work and, above all, a stubborn and professional mindset to complete the assignment successfully no matter what obstacles were to be surmounted to achieve success.

Technically speaking all pathfinders had to be proficient in selecting DZs for paratroopers, LZs for helicopters and landing strips for fixed-wing aircraft. Not only did they have to be able to select them in the required localities but they were also required to mark and man them, by day or night, and to take control of aircraft movement in and out of these air-controlled areas. Thus a parachute drop could be controlled from the ground with the team, acting as DZ controllers, giving banking instructions to para-dropping aircraft and even, if required, to order 'red light on', followed by 'green light on', especially at night when IPs (initial points) and dimensions of DZs are difficult to determine by aircrews.

And when it came to chopper LZs, I wanted my pathfinders to be able to select, mark and man them, again as controllers at any time, day or night, so that we would not experience another desperate scramble for seats as happened during the Cassinga operation when enemy tanks rolled onto the only LZ still available to extract the paratroopers after completion of the operation.

It followed therefore that the pathfinder organization essentially had to be a PF (Regular Army) organization. It would take far too long to train pathfinders to even think of using National Servicemen for this task. Training would entail down-to-earth training in small-unit tactics, bush craft and survival, tracking and anti-tracking, FAC (forward air control), advanced medics and first aid, HALO (high altitude, low opening—free-fall parachuting), combat-based ATC (air traffic control), DZ and LZ safety officers, weapons systems, advanced signalling including Morse code (still relevant in those days) and advanced driving and maintenance training to be able to deal with

breakdowns in the Sabres we were using within the pathfinder company.

I had decided that, under African conditions, the SAS-type Sabre would be the ideal vehicle to infiltrate pathfinder teams deep into Angola, the SWAPO guerrilla base area, which would increase the sustainability of pathfinder teams over a lengthy period of time deep inside enemy-dominated real estate. Enough logistics could be carried on board to keep a pathfinder detachment in the field for a month or more while also providing a formidable base of fire support should 'the mango hit the fan'. It could, of course, also be used to conduct highly effective raids on opportunity targets such as convoys, air fields or in support of parachute assaults because it had tremendous firepower at its disposal. However, other means of infiltration could also be used to deploy, especially, small teams of pathfinders, such as HALO parachuting, infiltrating on foot, by small boat or even air-landed by chopper behind enemy lines.

Because these men had to be regulars (PF) it presented me with problems I could not readily solve since 44 Parachute Brigade was, essentially, a CF (reserve) formation. Part-time soldiering for pathfinders could not even be contemplated and creating a regular force within a reserve force would be like turning water into wine. Fortunately Chief of the Army, General Viljoen, inadvertently came to my rescue. A hostage situation in a bank in Pretoria suddenly materialized which called for the police to deploy their special anti-hostage squad, which they did rather successfully. For some reason General Viljoen decided that we, too, should have our own anti-hostage squad in the army. He called me in and ordered me to get a Permanent Force (PF) one off the ground as soon as possible. This, of course, was duplicating an already existing capability but I held my tongue because I suddenly was presented with the required gap to start recruiting for my pathfinder company.

Fortuitously I was summoned by the Director Army Operations and instructed to develop a so-called Q-Car to fool SWAPO into attacking a presumed 'civilian' vehicle only to find machine guns popping up from its 'innards' to wipe them out. This worked well in Rhodesia where attacks on civilian vehicles and buses were frequent but it would not work in the operational area because SWAPO rarely, if ever, attacked civilian vehicles. They had, however, been brave enough to attack military vehicles from time to time. Money was, nevertheless, granted to see the project through. This created another gap I could exploit, with the aid of Dr Vernon Joynt at CSIR, to develop our own SAS-styled Sabre. The Director General Army Operations did not know the difference between a Q-Car and a Sabre anyway.

Then, as a final coincidence, the old Rhodesia, through betrayal, came to an end when the monstrous misfit, Robert Mugabe, took over from Bishop Abel Muzorewa after deliberately rigged elections. Suddenly a number of former Rhodesian regular soldiers were left without a job, under possible threat from the Mugabe government and with nowhere to go. I, therefore, grasped the opportunity to use this splendid reservoir of combat-experienced operators to fill my 'anti-hostage' squad, aka the pathfinder company, with combat-experienced former members from the RLI (Rhodesian Light Infantry), the Selous Scouts and the SAS.

They, however, had to do another selection course based on SAS procedures; to weed out any chancers and all had to go through another 'South African' basic parachute course. Some, like 'Frenchy', did it for the third or fourth time in their military careers! After that followed training in small-team operations on the Limpopo River under the auspices of WOII McAleese, a former 22SAS member, and then bush craft and survival in the Western Caprivi. Courses with the South African Air Force were lined up to make all pathfinders highly skilled, inter-service operators in the field of army-air force combined operations.

I personally took the pathfinder company to Owamboland and into Angola to introduce them to a somewhat different counter-guerrilla style of warfare. SWAPO was more aggressive than their ZANLA or even their Matabele-based ZIPRA counterparts. We had some exciting contacts which will no doubt be described with some detail in this book. They stayed for a while on the border, deliberately so, because I wanted to prove their worth particularly to the commander and staff of Sector 10. Brigadier Badenhorst, OC of Sector 10 and a soldier with an inbuilt animosity toward anybody who spoke the Queen's American, Rhodesian, Australian or even South African English, hated the very sight of us, however, and especially when the small pathfinder company started to achieve significant operational results while his much larger subordinate units struggled to achieve anything beyond the mediocre.

Unfortunately my days as commander of 44 Parachute Brigade were cut short and thus the further development of the pathfinder company was also put on the backburner by the new commander. I had been manoeuvred into an intolerable and undeserved situation by three one-dimensional generals (and some brigadiers) until I was confronted by General Geldenhuys, then Chief of The Army to make a choice of wherever else I could be fitted into the SADF pattern of service as long as it was not with 44 Parachute Brigade! I thus left the brigade under a cloud with a major mission still unfulfilled, i.e. to develop the pathfinder company into what was my vision for them. Thus the pathfinder company withered away because only a few of the original pathfinders renewed their contracts under the new management.

Nevertheless we had some good times together. This is their book; a collection of stories about the founding and deployment of a unit of basically 'Foreign Legionnaires' from different parts of the world who had become welded together into a most aggressive and remarkable combat unit, unsurpassed by any other SADF units in their positive and aggressive approach to battle. For me it was an honour to have faced incoming lead together with them. They, like I, have advanced in years but the memories are still fresh in our minds.

To all my former pathfinders, I want to say thank you for your comradeship, your support in and out of battle and for the ties which were forged then and which are still unbreakable today.

Colonel Jan D. Breytenbach VRD, SD, SM, MMM

Glossary

2IC	second-in-command
AA	anti-aircraft
AAA	anti-aircraft artillery
AFB	air force base
braaivleis	barbeque
brown jobs	colloquial term for the army (*also* the browns)
casevac	common abbreviation for casualty evacuation
CF	Citizen Force (Reserve / Territorial Army)
cheesemine	name used to describe the communist-manufactured anti-vehicle mine shaped like a large, round cheese
chimurenga	war of liberation (from the 1896 Mashona uprising in Rhodesia)
CO	commanding officer
cut line	the border fence between Angola and South West Africa
dagga	colloquial term for marijuana or cannabis
dominee	priest (Afrikaans)
doppies	expended cartridge cases (Afrikaans)
DZ	drop zone
FAC	forward air controller
FAPLA	*Forças Armadas Populares de Libertação de Angola* (People's Armed Forces for the Liberation of Angola)
flatdog	colloquial term for crocodile
Flossie	affectionate name given to the C-130 / C-160 transport aircraft that linked the border war with South Africa
FM	frequency modulation
FNLA	*Frente Nacional para a Libertação de Angola* (National Front for the Liberation of Angola)
FUP	form-up point
gomo	small, rounded hills which dot the Rhodesian / Zimbabwean landscape
GPS	global position system
HE	high explosive
HF	high frequency radio transmissions
hondo	battle, war (Shona)
hooch	bivouac

IV	intravenous
LZ	landing zone (for helicopters)
MAG	*Mitrailleuse d'Appui General*, 7.62 x 51mm general-purpose machine gun
manne	affectionate Afrikaans term referring to the men of the same unit
mielie / mealie	corn on the cob or maize
mielie pap	maize meal
MID	Mentioned in Dispatches
mkhulu	Zulu word of respect, describing an old man
MPLA	*Movimento Popular de Libertação de Angola* (Popular Movement for the Liberation of Angola)
NCO	non-commissioned officer
NS	national service / serviceman
OC	officer commanding
OP	observation post
PAC	Pan Africanist Congress
Parabat	Parachute Battalion
PF	Permanent Force (Regular Army)
PLAN	People's Liberation Army of Namibia (armed wing of SWAPO)
recce	reconnaissance
Rhodesia	former name of Zimbabwe. Previously a British colony and self-governing state in the Commonwealth until Prime Minister Ian Smith severed ties with Britain with his Unilateral Declaration of Independence in 1965. What began as civil unrest in 1962 culminated in a lengthy insurgency war, with guerrilla raids on farmers, missionaries, clerics and other civilians. After a negotiated settlement, the country was granted formal independence from Britain in 1980 and changed its name to Zimbabwe
RLI	Rhodesian Light Infantry
RPG-7	rocket-propelled grenade: anti-tank, tube-launched grenade of Russian origin, having a maximum effective range of 800 metres, and an explosive warhead weighing 2.4kg. It is robust, soldier-proof, easy to use, and was much favoured by SWAPO
RSA	Republic of South Africa
RV	rendezvous
SAAF	South African Air Force
SADF	South African Defence Force

SAP	South African Police
SAS	Special Air Service
shona	an open area in the bush that fills with water during the rainy season, and is invariably dry during the winter months
sjambok	cow-hide whip
SOP	standard operating procedure
spec ops	special operations
spoor	tracks, trails, signs
SWA	South West Africa, formerly a German colony, now known as Namibia
SWAPO	South West Africa People's Organization—a misnomer as the organization largely represented only the Owambo people, the largest ethnic group in Namibia. It became that country's ruling party when the territory gained independence in March 1990
takkies	slang for plimsolls or athletic-styled trainer shoes
terr	terrorist
tiffie	mechanic
TT	tamed / turned terrorist
u/s	unserviceable
uitlander	foreigner (Afrikaans)
UNITA	*União Nacional para a Independência Total de Angola* (National Union for the Total Independence of Angola)
VHF	very high frequency radio, limited to line-of-sight communication
vlei	low-lying swampy area
WO	warrant officer (class I or II)
Yati Strip	the international border of Angola and South West Africa between the Cunene and Kavango rivers consisted of a straight, graded strip, 420 kilometres in length, with the original barrier being a four-strand, barbed-wire fence. One kilometre south of the border another parallel strip was graded. The land between these two cleared lines was known as the Yati Strip. Originally the strip held a no-go significance, but by the later stages of the war this was almost totally ignored by all
ZANLA	Zimbabwe National Liberation Army (armed wing of ZANU)
ZANU	Zimbabwe African National Union
ZAPU	Zimbabwe African People's Union
ZIPRA	Zimbabwe People's Revolutionary Army (armed wing of ZAPU)

Chapter 1
Formation

Southern Africa in 1980

The Pathfinder Company, 44 Parachute Brigade was born in 1980 out of the death throes of Rhodesia, and this conflict like all others of the period was coloured by the Cold War. The standoff between East and West dominated world politics as the two sides engaged in an ever-frightening arms race to gain advantage over the other.

Those in the West, the NATO countries of North America and Western Europe, saw themselves as free, progressive and enlightened. The Warsaw Pact countries of Eastern Europe were looked upon as enslaved and controlled. The Soviets for reasons best known to themselves built the Berlin Wall and isolated themselves behind what Sir Winston Churchill called the 'Iron Curtain'. They engaged in subversive activity to promote their communist beliefs and attack Western influence. The Chinese under Mao Tse Tong likewise spared no expense to attack the West and to promote their own brand of communism.

Wherever in the world a dissatisfied population wanted to protest a colonial master or a Western-leaning government they were assured of funds, training and weapons to advance their protests to full revolution. Prior to 1980 a number of southern African countries had taken this route to gain a change of government or independence. Great Britain had successfully granted a relatively peaceful independence to Zambia, Malawi and Tanzania, but the Portuguese colonies of Angola and Mozambique descended into messy wars of terror and suffering. Both China and the Soviet Union were fully engaged in advising and arming the revolutionary forces.

The Rhodesian bush war took a different path to its neighbours because the white population, who were essentially 'locals' and not ex-patriots as in other colonies, mounted such a vigorous and successful campaign against the insurgent communist terrorists. However, by 1980 it was obvious to all that the enormous cost in lives could not be sustained, and with the ending of South African support, peace at any price was desirable. Elections put the Marxist Comrade Robert Mugabe in control of the renamed Zimbabwe.

A Western observer might not appreciate the tribal nature of African politics. Mugabe's party ZANU (Zimbabwe African National Union) was supported by the Mashona tribe, while the Ndebele supported the rival ZAPU (Zimbabwe African People's Union). Once Mugabe was sure in his position

SWAPO

By the early 1960s Sam Nujoma's SWAPO (South West Africa People's Organization) had emerged as the prominent nationalist party opposing the government in South West Africa. Their primary support base was drawn from the Owambo tribe in the north of the country. By 1966, terrorist actions against South West African and South African targets heralded a new phase in their revolution. SWAPO was a Marxist party, backed by the Soviet Union and liberal Western countries, mainly Scandinavian. Cadres were trained in the USSR, East Germany and Tanzania under Eastern Bloc instructors.

Direct action by the police and SADF drove the terrorists out of the country to safe havens in Angola where the Marxist MPLA afforded them sanctuary and support. SWAPO were absolutely ruthless in their modus operandi: torture and murder were common, and the laying of landmines indiscriminately caused many hundreds of innocent casualties. However, as fighters, SWAPO guerrillas were renowned for their aggressive qualities, more so than their Zimbabwean ZANLA and ZIPRA counterparts. SWAPO's military wing was grandly known as PLAN (People's Liberation Army of Namibia) but the pathfinders never used the name, so for consistency the term SWAPO is used throughout this book.

he sent his North Korean-trained Fifth Brigade into Matabeleland where an estimated 30,000 Ndebele civilians were massacred between 1982 and 1984.

In South Africa the Xhosa tribe of Nelson Mandela backed the ANC (African National Congress) and were often in violent confrontation with the Zulus of the rival Inkatha Freedom Party. The terrorist attacks on civilians carried out in South Africa by the ANC and the smaller PAC (Pan Africanist Congress) were not on the scale of the countries to the north and despite USSR support the revolt never developed into open warfare.

The government, controlled by the white Afrikaner National Party, were fully aware of the injustices of their apartheid policy, but wanted change to come at a manageable pace that did not destabilize the country. The ANC leader Nelson Mandela had been sent to prison for a life term in 1964 for terrorism, but by 1980 the government knew he was the man they would have to negotiate with to bring a change agreeable to the black majority. He was offered freedom if he renounced violence, but he refused and so remained in prison.

South West Africa (SWA), later to be called Namibia, was a protectorate of South Africa under a United Nations mandate, following the defeat of the original colonial power, Germany, after the First World War. SWA was fighting its own terrorist war against SWAPO (South West Africa People's Organization), the revolutionary party made up primarily of Owambo tribesmen. In order to counter the terror tactics of this organization the Pathfinder Company deployed to South West Africa. Here it operated mainly into Angola to destroy SWAPO bases and training camps.

It may be a Hollywood cliché for a soldier to 'save the last bullet for yourself', but to the pathfinders it was

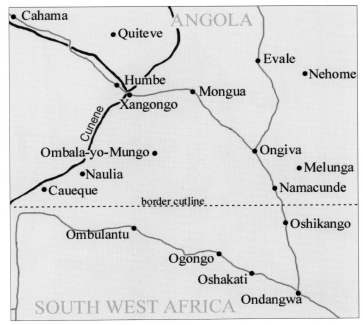

Southern Africa, 1980.

The border area of South West Africa and Angola. The operational area of Sector 10 had its headquarters at Oshakati. The SAAF airfield and the pathfinders' main camp were at Ondangwa.

an unwritten requirement; the alternative being torture, mutilation and a slow, lingering death. In the normal course of events soldiers in African wars did not take prisoners, nor did they expect to be taken prisoner. A terrorist could hand himself in and be dealt with according to the laws of the land, but once combat had started, it only ended with one side dead or fled. From the first recorded history, wars on the continent have been barbaric. As black Bantu tribes migrated south from the Congo Basin toward the end of the first millennium AD, they displaced, either by assimilation or genocide, the native Bushmen and Hottentots, and every tribal conflict, war and revolution since then has been marked by massacres and atrocities. The volunteers of the Pathfinder Company were well aware of that and were prepared to fight by those rules.

It is argued that 'one man's terrorist is another man's freedom fighter'. The pathfinders had no doubt about this. If an armed gang lived to advance their cause by terrorizing the local population, then they were terrorists. If they ambushed a farmer's wife while driving her children to school, they were terrorists. If they went into a village and rounded up the headman and witchdoctor, bayoneted their children, raped and mutilated their wives, then burned down the huts with the villagers inside, they were terrorists. If they went into a school, killed the teachers and marched the pupils hundreds of miles to training camps across the border, they were terrorists. The freedom fighter argument is left to those hand-wringing student romantics who have not seen the many parts that a human body can be blown into, nor have they heard the screams of the suffering, nor smelt the stench of fear.

Colonel Breytenbach giving directions to his American driver Lang Price. Navigation in Angola was by aerial photograph. As the Officer Commanding 44 Parachute Brigade he might have been content to sit behind a desk, but he formed the Pathfinder Company and its flying column, to take the war to SWAPO.

When Mugabe took control of Zimbabwe in April 1980, he united the so-called Frontline States against South Africa: Angola in the west, Zimbabwe and Zambia in the centre and Mozambique and Tanzania in the east, forming a band of mainly Marxist revolutionary states with a hatred of the wealthy and powerful white government of South Africa.

Using covert units, the SADF (South African Defence Force) supported the pro-Western dissident group Renamo (*Resistência Nacional Moçambicana*, the National Resistance Movement of Mozambique) in Mozambique, but it was in Angola that the Pathfinder Company operated and here the SADF gave crucial aid to UNITA (*União Nacional para a Independência Total de Angola*, the National Union for the Total Independence of Angola), a pro-Western group at war with the MPLA (*Movimento Popular de Libertação de Angola* (Popular Movement for the Liberation of Angola) government and its army FAPLA (*Forças Armadas Populares de Libertação de Angola*, the People's Armed Forces for the Liberation of Angola).

Much of southern Angola was under UNITA control and South African soldiers often found themselves ordered deep into Angola to combat FAPLA and the massive Cuban force which had been dispatched by Fidel Castro to prop up the fragile MPLA government. It was Cuban military might which ultimately brought FAPLA victory in the messy civil war. SADF attacks into Angola were mounted from South West Africa where they were already deployed in counter-terrorist operations against SWAPO.

Recruiting begins

Reserve airborne forces of the British Territorial Army were brigaded into 44 Parachute Brigade up until 1978 when it was disbanded in a reorganization exercise. In the same year the South Africans organized their own reserve airborne forces into a newly formed 44 Parachute Brigade, initially at Bloemfontein, then at its permanent home at Murrayhill, 25 miles north of Pretoria on the N1 Highway. 1 Parabat (Parachute Battalion) consisted of men doing their two years' National Service with a PF (Permanent Force) staff. The battalion maintained its independent role, but once National Service was completed these men then carried on their yearly call-up commitment

Rhodesian Light Infantry

While the military backgrounds of the candidates for the Pathfinder Company were rich and varied, the majority came from the Rhodesian Light Infantry, a regiment made famous for its hard fighting during the bush war that ravaged Rhodesia prior to the creation of Zimbabwe in 1980. Formed in 1961 as a white regiment at a time when Africa was in turmoil—murder and massacre marked colonial struggles—and the British government was hastily shedding the remnants of its empire, recruits were initially drawn from Rhodesia, South Africa and Great Britain, and trained by British instructors. As the seeds of revolution spread to Rhodesia operations against Marxist terrorists saw the RLI increasingly involved in the fighting and by the height of the war in 1977–79, the single-battalion regiment was permanently deployed in the bush at the forefront of hostilities. By then, as well as loyal Rhodesians, the ranks were filled with foreigners from other Commonwealth countries, USA and Europe—a total of 18 different nationalities were recorded in the ranks in 1979. The RLI perfected the Fireforce technique—a slick airborne and airmobile total envelopment of the enemy—of parachute-trained commandos based at forward airfields, deploying by ageing Alouette III helicopters and para-C-47 Dakotas to sightings of terrorists. Contact with the enemy was constant; it was possible for an RLI trooper to achieve two, sometimes three, operational parachute descents in a single day. The nicknames of the RLI speak volumes about them as a fighting force: 'The Saints' and 'The Incredibles'. This reputation was not achieved without cost: the regiment lost 135 men killed in action but accounted for an estimated 12,000 ZANLA and ZIPRA enemy guerrillas in its short 19-year history.

with 2 Parabat or 3 Parabat as part of the reservist CF (Citizen Force). These two battalions, together with the headquarters contingent and supporting arms constituted 44 Parachute Brigade.

The character of the brigade could not help but be a reflection of its colourful and controversial commander, Colonel Jan Breytenbach DVR, SD, SM, MMM. The colonel started his military career in tanks in the South African Army in 1950. He left in 1955 and joined the Fleet Air Arm of the British Royal Navy as a navigator and took part in the Suez landings in 1956. In 1961 he rejoined the South African Army and became a paratrooper. He was involved in covert operations in neighbouring 'problem' countries and was the founding commander of 1 Reconnaissance Commando. Some knew him as 'The Brown Man' due to his deep suntan caused by a lifetime spent in the bush. In 1975 he created 32 Battalion, which he forged in battle from the pro-Western FNLA (*Frente Nacional para a Libertação de Angola* (National Front for the Liberation of Angola) guerrilla forces during the South African intervention in Angola. Then came his involvement with 44 Parachute Brigade.

Colonel Breytenbach commanded the successful 1978 assault on SWAPO's main base at Cassinga in Angola, which was one of the largest airborne assaults anywhere since the Second World War. Apart from one rifle platoon and the mortar platoon from 1 Parabat the attacking infantry consisted of CF paratroopers from 44 Parachute Brigade. This large-scale raid set the pattern of operations to come and was yet another success for the colonel. Afrikaners in general and more so the military have often been criticized for having a narrow, blinkered view of things, and as a result Colonel Breytenbach's unorthodox approach to operations and his love of combat did not always sit well with his superiors with whom relations could be strained to say the least.

A lesson learned from the Cassinga attack was the need for pathfinders to head the airborne deployment. It was the role of pathfinders to be on the ground before the para drop, to mark out the drop zone, and to maintain

44 Parachute Brigade Headquarters was at Murrayhill, north of Pretoria. With no buildings other than the old farm sheds, accommodation was in tents.

The training camp at Mabalique was used to train and prepare the men for their selection test. Devoid of comforts the candidates made their home in any trench or bunker available. Ken Gaudet found himself living in a section of concrete piping. The ground sloped down to the Limpopo River, where on the far bank was the hostile country of Zimbabwe.

Candidates Rob Gilmour and Lang Price give orders for a camp attack exercise. All the men were given leadership training and were expected to plan and command fighting patrols.

Company Sergeant-Major Peter McAleese in one of his less conciliatory moments. The course drugged his drinks with Valium in order to escape his relentless training schedule, but he produced the finest trained and motivated group of soldiers who held him in the highest regard.

communications with the aircraft, directing them onto their correct targets. Once the paratroopers were on the ground the pathfinders would then assemble and marshall the disoriented paras to begin their operations.

Colonel Breytenbach's wish to form a pathfinder company became possible in April 1980. With the fall of neighbouring Rhodesia to the Marxist Mugabe, a pool of battle-experienced and highly competent soldiers were enlisting into the SADF and the colonel directed the cream towards 44 Parachute Brigade. The men were enrolled into the Permanent Force on a one-year 'short service' contract; they received normal rates of pay but were given a 500-rand bonus on joining and another R1,000 on completion of the contract.

One of the first recruits was a man with an already known reputation, Peter McAleese. A tough Glasgow upbringing prepared Peter for the Parachute Regiment and the SAS (twice), with whom he served in Aden during Britain's troubled pullout and Borneo during the Emergency. He was picked as part of a training team sent to Guyana, and left the army as a staff sergeant with a love and thorough knowledge of soldiering in general and combat in particular. In 1976 Peter commanded a group of British mercenaries working for the pro-western FNLA in Angola until the MPLA and their Cuban allies defeated them and the FNLA fell by the wayside. The following year he joined the Rhodesian SAS and for two years was involved in heavy combat before moving to Special Branch to run a unit of surrendered, or 'turned' terrorists. Joining 44 Para Brigade in June 1980 as a colour sergeant he was quickly promoted to Warrant Officer Class II and appointed Company Sergeant-Major to the Pathfinder Company with the task of selecting and training men to fill its ranks.

During the selection phase of the training in the majestic setting of the Drakensberg Mountains the candidates had to navigate between fixed points; strict time limits and weighted equipment demanded the highest standard of fitness and determination of the successful soldiers. Those who failed the test either filled jobs at Brigade Headquarters or were posted to one of the South African infantry battalions.

The Officer Commanding the Pathfinder Company was Captain Botes, a PF para officer who had a long association with Colonel Breytenbach. He had much combat experience in Angola, including being wounded and left for dead when he had to make his way back to South West Africa alone and hurt. He, together with CSM McAleese, planned training for the new arrivals, training that would culminate with a selection course only the toughest and most dedicated soldiers would pass. The first 23 foreign candidates found that a high level of fitness was expected. Battle drills were carried out using only live ammunition; the purpose of this demanding routine was to weed out those not up to the task and to prepare the remainder for battle in Angola.

Assisting with the training was another famous soldier who had found his way to 44 Parachute Brigade: WOII Dennis Croukamp BCR was a Rhodesian with a formidable fighting reputation. After starting his National Service he joined up in 1965 as a regular soldier in the Rhodesian Light Infantry and was awarded the Bronze Cross of Rhodesia in 1970 for bravery carried out during a contact with a terrorist gang in the Zambezi Valley in 1968 during Operation Cauldron. 'Crouks' continued up the promotion ladder until he took the selection course for the Selous Scouts where he excelled on small-team recce patrols into Mozambique.

Slightly stooped shoulders meant that he would not be a 'parade ground soldier' but that was more than made up for by his love of the bush and he was never out of action throughout his military career. Crouks returned to the RLI in 1979 as Recce Troop commander before being promoted to Commando Sergeant-Major, Support Commando. Then the time came to turn his back on his old country and move to South Africa.

The squad candidates for selection moved to a training camp on the banks of the Limpopo River, which formed South Africa's northern border. The now-hostile country of Zimbabwe was only a hundred yards over the trickling river shrunken by the winter drought. The camp, called Mabalique, consisted of a couple of basic brick buildings and various lean-tos, so the men had to find trenches and hovels to make their homes.

To get to the camp it was necessary to go through a gate in the security fence. This barrier consisted of two high wire fences with prickly sisal plants growing thickly between them; it ran the whole length of the international border

Above: In majestic surroundings Sergeant Gilly Gillmore gives comfort to an exhausted Pete Morpuss who has just completed a leg of the endurance test: broken in body but not in spirit.

Below: At the Parachute School, Bloemfontein: Lang Price, Ken Gaudet and Rob Gilmour, all para-trained ex-members of Support Commando, RLI. For Ken Gaudet this was the third para course he had attended.

Above: Trainees lined up prior to boarding the para Dakotas on the runway. The National Servicemen are on the right in white jump suits; the pathfinders are on the left in their brown coveralls. Though the National Servicemen were told not to mix with these strangers it quickly became known who these foreigners were.

Right: A training para drop.

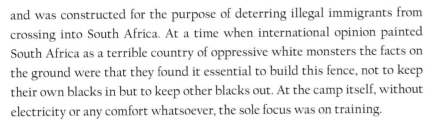

and was constructed for the purpose of deterring illegal immigrants from crossing into South Africa. At a time when international opinion painted South Africa as a terrible country of oppressive white monsters the facts on the ground were that they found it essential to build this fence, not to keep their own blacks in but to keep other blacks out. At the camp itself, without electricity or any comfort whatsoever, the sole focus was on training.

For months this high level of preparation continued, each candidate being brought up to junior NCO standard, involved with planning patrols, giving orders and preparing briefings, as well as leading camp attacks, ambushes and anti-ambush drills; weapon familiarization was practised with the full range of western and communist weapons. Every aspect of bush warfare was covered by a schedule so demanding that the pathfinder candidates found it necessary to spike CSM McAleese's drinks with valium in order to get some respite. In a short time a confidence and mutual regard developed among the men at Mabalique that remained with them throughout their service and beyond.

The weapons handled during the training consisted of the usual selection of Soviet and Chinese assault rifles, SKS, AK, AKM, plus RPK and RPD machine guns. The rifles carried by the men during their physical training were ex-Rhodesian folding-butt FNs; these were still painted in the usual Rhodesian camouflage pattern and were weapons very familiar to the men. These rifles were claimed to have originally been captured in Zambia during a

raid by the Rhodesian SAS and brought down to South Africa by Pete McAleese. For the tactical live-firing training they used the South African R4 rifle, and this was something new to them. Copied from the Israeli Galil rifle its 5.56mm calibre was not popular with the men who wanted the knock-down power of the old FN 7.62mm bullet. One American went so far as to refuse to carry the R4, taking on operations his trusty FN and carrying his own supply of ammunition.

This first group all had previous parachute training and experience so after being driven back to Murrayhill for two days they then travelled by train to the parachute school at Bloemfontein to complete a five-day refresher course. They were issued jumpsuits and introduced to the 'marble'; a concrete block which they had to carry around the hanger and training area at all times. Considering the ammo box they had been training with for eight weeks this was just something else to get used to.

During the training they made seven jumps from a DC-3, the old Second World War vintage Dakotas they had been used to operating from in Rhodesia, and C-160 Transalls. All passed the course and were presented with para wings to wear on their shirts and the Parabat beret badge.

The finale of the training phase was the selection course held according to SAS criteria. CSM McAleese planned routes in the Drakensberg Mountains along which the men had to carry weighted rucksacks in timed stages; names like Giant's Castle, Monk's Cowl, Champagne Peak and Cathedral Peak, so familiar to adventurous tourists were now to be painfully engraved in the minds of the candidates. The failure to navigate the route or arrive within the allotted time meant dismissal from the Pathfinder Company. These mountains in Natal are a most beautiful and dramatic region of grey, mist-enshrouded hills, but they are also the scene of some of the coldest, wettest and most miserable weather in all Africa

The one thing the pathfinders remembered most from this harrowing experience was the 80lb ammunition box they had to carry. This wooden box with short rope handles was extremely heavy and extremely awkward to manhandle; of course designed to be an added aggravation to an already stressful experience. Seventeen men eventually passed this test so that by November 1980 the Pathfinder Company finally existed in more than name.

On returning to Murrayhill they found another two dozen or so new arrivals ready to start their ordeal; these men like the first were all foreigners, mostly but not all friends from the RLI. The word was spreading along the grapevine that there was a home for these fighting men. During the last days of Rhodesia just about all the regular soldiers in the army had applied to join the SADF at a new recruiting office set up in Salisbury. The talk in the RLI was that 32 Battalion was the combat outfit to join, and indeed it was, but the few places for white officers and NCOs quickly absorbed the first recruits. The SAS and Selous Scout operators were guaranteed a place in the Recce Commandos so it left the others at a loose end, until Colonel Breytenbach came to the rescue.

Conditions at Murrayhill were only marginally better than Mabalique. The dilapidated farmhouse that stood on the site prior to the SADF buying the land provided the only solid building; the old house and outbuildings were now the offices for the brigade, whereas a tent city was constructed for the CF personnel of 2 Parabat and 3 Parabat who had been recently called up and were rehearsing for a parade to receive colours for the first time.

A visitor to the camp would first notice the lack of buildings, and secondly the fit bronzed young men engaged in various outdoor tasks, their muscled bodies stripped down only to shorts which in the 1970s and early '80s were styled tight and very short.

"So, these are the famous Parabats?"

"No, they are the JWs."

On the successful completion of the course the pathfinders were awarded their para beret badges and wings to wear on their shirts over the left breast pocket.

'JWs' (Jehovah's Witnesses) was the generic term for conscientious objectors. Rather than complete two years National Service followed by annual call-ups, these men chose to serve a prison sentence in Spartan conditions after which they were free to continue their uninterrupted careers. Daily, a party of JWs was delivered to the camp to carry out menial jobs; it gave them a chance to be out of prison and they 'happily' undertook non-military type work. Jobs were defined as military or non-military and mutually agreed upon beforehand between prisoners and guards.

The Brigade Sergeant-Major was WOI Muller, an Afrikaner who was close to retirement. He had seen it, been there and done that and treated everyone like his son. A genuinely nice man respected by all.

One house was eventually set aside for the Pathfinder Company but newcomers had to persevere in tents which flooded in the heavy summer rainstorms. Their camp consequently became known as 'the swamp'. Electricity was provided by a generator maintained by a local man whose job was to run it from 6 o'clock in the morning until 10 at night, a task he magnificently failed to execute on many occasions.

The water supply would often fail, leaving nothing for washing and sanitation, with water for the cookhouse being collected from outside the camp by bowser. The fact that the men received stoppages of pay for food and accommodation was an added irritant, and also an incentive to get up to the border where there would be no such deductions. The married soldiers fared better and lived on a purpose-built estate in fully furnished mobile homes in the Pretoria suburb of Lyttleton. Their accommodation was comfortable and a daily bus service ran the men to the camp.

Because this was a brigade of reservists there was not a great number of personnel needed in the normal course of a working day, with the few driving and administrative tasks in the brigade being carried out by ex-Rhodesian force members who found themselves quite at home ... except for the one big difference from their previous service: the lack of batmen. In the RLI, in order to keep the men free to fight, black civilian servants did all the menial tasks in barracks and in the bush camps: cooking, laundry and cleaning. Now they found themselves back in an army where the soldier was responsible for doing everything himself. The low standard of the food was another cause of complaint but none of this mattered if the promise of active service was fulfilled.

It was, and the Pathfinder Company was divided into three groups and assigned various tasks: two went into combat and the third started an international incident.

Chapter 2
Q-Car, Cuamato and Mabalique

Q-Car

In early December 1980 the first small group of pathfinders flew by Transall C-160 from Pretoria to Ondangwa in South West Africa. This part of the SWA/Angola border was configured in a straight line drawn on a map, running east-west; physically it was marked on the ground by a dirt road with a wire fence on the Angolan side. The region was part of Owamboland and was what the military designated as Sector 10 operational area. The sector headquarters was at the town of Oshakati, with the main SAAF airfield a short drive southeast at Ondangwa.

The colonel and a Parabat sergeant, Theunis Kruger, travelled to the operational area with the first group of pathfinders who were under the command of WOII Dennis Croukamp. The group included Ken Gaudet, Jay, Mike Landskov, Jean-Luk 'Frenchie' Busmey, Mark Griffiths and Dean Shelly. On the flight the pathfinders became acquainted with some new men who would be working with the company and who would significantly change their method of operating: Englishmen WOII Frank Green and Staff Sergeant Ken William, and Rhodesian Sergeant Frankie King.

Brigadier Badenhorst and the people at Sector 10 headquarters did not know exactly what to do with the rogue Colonel Breytenbach and his band of buccaneers, so to keep them low-profile they were shuffled about from camp to camp. Starting off at the Ondangwa airbase they were then sent to out-of-the-way camps at Meersup and Okotopi. The colonel attributed this hostility to the brigadier's Broederbonder mentality, a dislike for anything foreign and especially these English-speaking paratroopers.

Okotopi was typical of the small patrol base camps built by the South Africans. An infantry company on border security duty was in residence at each of these camps, from where they patrolled their designated area of their responsibility. The low living standards at Murrayhill and Mabalique had prepared the pathfinders for yet more discomfort at Okotopi. The make-up of these camps was a simple square fort with the white earthen outer walls bulldozed up into embankments to provide protection from small-arms fire; while inside the camp universal green canvas tents provided accommodation. At the camp was a unit of mounted infantry who did their patrols on horseback. The pathfinders gauged their welcome by the fact that they were allocated tents positioned between the cookhouse, the horse lines and the toilet tent.

Uniform

On duty in South Africa the regulation nutria-brown SADF uniform was worn with the cherry-coloured para beret. The long-sleeved shirt was supposed to be worn with the sleeves rolled up and the rank badge worn on a brassard but many pathfinders had the shirts tailored and sleeves shortened with the rank chevrons sewn on, in the Rhodesian fashion. Because initial recruiting was done at Army Headquarters the volunteers might be badged differently: those who had recently done the parachute course wore the cloth Parabat winged badge; others, whether para trained or not, wore the infantry white metal springbok badge, but signals and engineers badges were also seen. The one difference from other SADF troops was that the coloured balkies, or 'candy bar' badges, were not worn below the regimental badge.

continued overleaf

33

On formal duty in South West Africa the same nutria-brown uniform was worn, but in the various camps shorts and T-shirts were normal; either the issue black shorts with brown T-shirts, or any Rhodesian or civilian pattern. If the pathfinders were deployed into Angola on their own or with 32 Battalion there was complete freedom of choice regarding uniform. They would leave camp correctly dressed then change into camo once in the bush away from friendly forces. The one-piece jumpsuit, like overalls, was popular at first but preference changed to the more convenient separate items. Thus brown combat jackets and trousers were 'mixed and matched' with Rhodesian or captured communist camouflage. Headwear was either the issue brown floppy hat or a variety of camo caps. Brown leather, high-leg boots were normal issue and these, or *veldskoene* (suede bush shoes), were worn into combat. The one item of kit envied by the pathfinders was the spec-ops (special operations) boots worn by 32 Battalion: these were canvas-sided, high-leg boots which were more appropriate for the conditions, and brought certain kudos to the wearer. When on operations with other SADF units regulation brown uniforms were worn. Kevlar helmets were carried but seldom worn. Latterly the company operated in FAPLA uniforms captured during Operation Protea, with the men carrying AK-47s to complete the illusion of subterfuge.

The first of the pathfinders to deploy to South West Africa. This camp at Meersup was one of several where they were sent in order to keep them out of the way.

The toilets, it should be explained, were a result of the geology, as throughout the area rain did not soak into the earth but ran along the surface until it pooled at the famous Etosha Pan. Consequently, toilets consisted of a number of three-seater 'thunderboxes' placed within ablution tents where everyone could socialize while answering nature's call. At a particular time, usually when they were so full that the lids could not be closed, a 'honeysuckle' tanker lorry would arrive and suck out the contents.

In the camps the food for the National Servicemen was extremely poor, whereas the few PF personnel did rather better with their own dining tent and properly prepared meals. This then was the problem when the pathfinders arrived: all being PF they were entitled to the same consideration, but the initial novelty of these fighting *uitlanders* soon turned to dislike when it was realized they would eat all the officers' and NCOs' food and drink all the beer from their limited supply.

WOII Green had developed a 'Q-Car', using knowledge and experience gained in the Rhodesian bush war. He'd 'acquired' and converted a Land Rover with a hidden secret, and it travelled with the group on the aircraft. A common vehicle on African roads was the soft-skinned Land Rover. This particular one had masked protective armour plating and concealed general-purpose machine guns; the tyres were filled with a special liquid that would keep them inflated in case of bullet punctures. Inside the wheel hub of the spare tyre on the bonnet was an armour plate on which six steel tubes were welded at a slight angle to propel hand grenades from the vehicle. A small premeasured charge was placed under each steel tube in which standard hand grenades were set; the pins of the grenades were pulled, with the steel tubes just large enough for the grenades to be placed inside and still hold the lever down. After all six grenades were in place a simple paper cover was taped over it, with the end result of the whole affair looking like a normal spare tyre. There was also a device to fire eight shotgun barrels to the immediate front.

The Q-Car. A simple principle that had worked in Rhodesia: tempt the enemy out into the open with an easy-looking target then surprise him with devastating firepower.

Ex-US Special Forces Mike Landskov with one of the two machine guns that sprung up when the trap was activated; he received a bullet splinter wound to his hand when they were ambushed for real.

Out of sight, the crew in the back of the vehicle consisted of two machine gunners and two assistants, while in front sat the driver and escort. The guns were on a spring-loaded pedestal that would immediately move to a position above the protective enclosure on a prearranged signal or when an ambush occurred, and could be fired by the gunners. The machine guns, Belgian 7.62 x 51mm FN MAG 58s were linked to boxes containing 3,000 rounds of ammunition. The initial firepower was awesome and devastating.

Just before the pathfinders' arrival, a group of SWAPO terrorists had ambushed an ambulance and shot up two doctors before fading back into the scrub after a brief firefight. Luckily, the doctors were only slightly wounded. So it was now the task of the Q-Car patrol to present themselves for ambush and destroy the SWAPO gang. Tame terrorists (TTs, also 'turned' terrorists) who had changed sides were brought into the Q-Car plan but this left some of the pathfinders feeling somewhat uneasy.

After fine-tuning the operation of the Q-Car mechanisms and weapons, the plan, as prepared by the colonel, WOII Croukamp and Sergeant Kruger, was rehearsed and then put into action. The plain-looking and apparently defenceless Q-Car manned by concealed pathfinders visited the local community where Colonel Breytenbach, dressed as a priest, dished out Christmas presents and aid to the needy. Having established a peaceful presence in the area, the vehicle, over the next few weeks, travelled at the same regular time on the one major tarred road that ran past Ondangwa, to Oshakati in the north and the main supply depot at Grootfontein in the south. By creating a pattern they presented an opportunity too good for the terrorists to resist and, as well as spreading the word that they were carrying Christmas goodies, they added an escort of two Buffel armoured troop-carriers with soldiers from 1 Parabat aboard for good measure. Finally, one evening the inevitable happened.

Pathfinder Ken Gaudet was a Vietnam veteran from the 173rd Airborne Brigade, and had served in Support Commando, RLI before becoming one of the first to pass pathfinder selection. He later recalled his experience of the contact:

I was driving the second escort Buffel, approximately 25 metres behind the Q-Car. As we began to enter the kraal that was right along the road, I saw a single green tracer. I immediately began to slow the vehicle when all of a sudden I was temporarily blinded by a bright ring of fire in front of me. There was a loud explosion and all around our vehicle could be heard the *ping* and whine of passing shrapnel. The Q-Car had set off the grenades and opened up on the enemy position. Even with the noise and confusion it was clearly determined where the terrorist fire was coming from, and the Q-Car was raking the enemy position with devastating machine-gun fire.

I could see movement on the sides of the road; the terrs were trying to manoeuvre into position out of the line of fire from the Q-Car and toss grenades into it. This is where the escort vehicle came into play. From our position on the road the paras were firing at likely targets of opportunity and enemy muzzle flashes. The para officer in my vehicle directed one of his troopers to put some illumination flares overhead and identify the target for the para RPG-7 operator—the building the terrs were firing from.

After two or three minutes of small-arms fire and a few RPG rounds the enemy building was in flames and our paras were getting out of the vehicle to move into a position to sweep through the contact area and look for any sign of terrorist activity.

During the sweep four dead terrs were found in the building and numerous blood spoor [trails] were detected. We captured three AK-47 assault rifles and one RPD machine gun. Our sweep group also found where the enemy had dug shell scrapes, which convinced us that this was a planned ambush to take out our convoy.

In the midst of the attack Jay saw a terrorist throw a grenade which landed under Ken's Buffel. He shouted for Ken to stay inside, but not hearing the shout in the confusion Ken dismounted as the grenade detonated, damaging the vehicle but Ken was miraculously unharmed. During the mopping-up operations he noticed that Colonel Breytenbach was bleeding from a shrapnel wound to his neck which he bandaged with a field dressing. Mike Landskov also picked up a shrapnel wound to his hand—all in all, a small cost for such a good result.

With the element of surprise now gone the value of the Q-Car was diminished, and patrolling continued for a while but without the same enthusiasm. There were frustrating periods of inactivity. Mike Landskov took rides on the resupply helicopter missions to 32 Battalion inside Angola to relieve the boredom. Sergeant Kruger took the TTs under his wing and developed his own anti-terrorist techniques. WOII Green and Sergeant King returned to Pretoria to prepare their next surprise for the pathfinders ... and SWAPO.

Cuamato

The SADF had decided not just to react to SWAPO action but to strike at their camps within Angola, to disrupt their organization and deal them a crippling blow before they even set foot into South West Africa. By doing so it reduced the effectiveness of their activities and allowed comparatively normal life and business to continue in SWA. So, sometime after the first pathfinder group had established their nomadic existence on the border, a second small group led by CSM McAleese set off by aircraft for Sector 10. These pathfinders were attached to a company of CF paras for a camp attack on Cuamato, a town 25 miles inside Angola.

Landmine incidents had been increasing: in 1980 alone there were 327. Military intelligence had discovered that gangs who had been laying mines indiscriminately in Owamboland, originated from Cuamato. Many innocent casualties had been caused and it was time to send the perpetrators a message.

As the pathfinders were about to find out SWAPO were better trained and better equipped than their previous enemy, ZANLA and ZIPRA, had been; not only did they have much larger weapons but they also had the determination to stand and fight. Regular FAPLA forces were also believed to be in residence in the town and giving full support to SWAPO.

A briefing was given, first in Afrikaans then translated into English for the benefit of the pathfinders who were distributed among the platoons of the Parabat C Company. Puma helicopters flew them to the attack forming-up point inside Angola, with Ken Gaudet and Frenchie Busmey in the second helicopter to land. The company then advanced by foot toward the town, the pathfinders loaded down with all the kit and ammunition their experience and training told them they would need, while the paras were more lightly

Ranks and appointments

The SADF was essentially a Citizen Force (CF), or Territorial Army, with National Servicemen initially called up for two year's duty and, on completion of their national service, moving onto a system of regular call-ups, or 'camps'. The full-time Permanent Force (PF), the regular army, provided the core of non-commissioned officers. The foreigners, or *uitlanders*, who were recruited into the Pathfinders were also PF and kept the rank they had held in their previous army. Those who had been private soldiers or who could not prove earlier service became lance-corporals. Thus the company was very rank-heavy, but small-team operations demanded that everyone in the field, no matter what his rank, had to share equally the guard and other mundane duties involved in combat operations.

Because of the unorthodox nature of the Pathfinder Company it could be thought that the lines between the officers and other ranks might have become blurred, or that these hard-core fighters were scornful of military protocol. This was never the case and correct etiquette was maintained throughout. In camp, officers were saluted and addressed as 'sir' as was their right, but in the field no badges of rank were worn and relations were less formal. Where a man had a particular skill or experience it sometimes happened that he would be given responsibility for a particular task over a soldier of a more senior rank; such was the nature of small-team operations.

Canadian Rob Gilmour and American Lang Price pose with an anti-tank rocket launcher. Rocket-propelled grenades were an invariable feature of contacts in southern Africa, resulting in many soldiers carrying shrapnel wounds.

equipped for an expected shorter engagement. It was hot, dry and dusty, and they expected at any moment to receive enemy fire as they approached the town, but it didn't happen. Searching the buildings it became clear that everyone—civilian, soldier and terrorist—had fled.

The advance to contact continued with C Company heading northward where the enemy had last been seen, with the forward section of the forward platoon straining to see through the bush that obscured their vision, when they spotted two enemy guerrillas to their front. They radioed the information to their lieutenant who then split his platoon into two groups, he moving forward with the lead group. About ten minutes later a wall of fire was suddenly opened on them. Everybody was down on the ground firing to the front; incoming fire was not only small arms but heavy machine guns and 82mm mortars. This was a camp with substantial defences.

The company was taking casualties but their orders were to carry on into the camp. The CSM was tasked by the platoon commander to storm the objective, so he and Canadian pathfinder Rob Gilmour, previously of the Canadian Army and Support Commando, RLI, with two volunteer paras made a mad dash across 150 yards of open ground while everyone else provided as much covering fire as they could. Convinced that their lives were now at an end it was something more than amazing that they covered the distance under a hail of bullets without anyone being hit.

Then the real fight began.

Finding themselves in among the trenches and bunkers it was desperate close-quarter killing. Suddenly two terrorists showed themselves outside a bunker and Gilmour shot them both dead before tossing a white phosphorus grenade into the bunker. Eventually the pathfinders went firm in these positions and provided covering fire for the next para assault on their right.

There was more hand-to-hand fighting as they penetrated farther into the camp where an inner network of trenches was hitting the paras with everything they had, including RPDs and 14.5 AA heavy machine guns, with even a terrifying 75mm recoilless rifle thrown into the fray. CSM McAleese's R4 rifle jammed as he confronted one SWAPO cadre whom he had to club with his rifle butt before the terrorist had a chance to shoot.

Gilmour was clearing trenches when he came upon a heavy machine-gun position. He and a CF NCO, Corporal Wessels, were boosted up, ready to toss grenades into the position as the gun opened up on them at point-blank range, missing Rob but taking off most of the corporal's head. The grenades, however, did the job and wiped out the gun crew.

Puma helicopters were used extensively to deploy troops and deliver supplies to patrols in Angola. On several occasions the pathfinders were moved to forward base camps and put on standby duty to support helicopter operations in Angola and Mozambique: in the event of an aircraft crash they would secure the area for recovery, but fortunately they were never required.

The nerve-wracking task of clearing bunkers and trenches continued apace, but by last light the enormous camp was still not fully in South African hands. They then received the order to withdraw: to their annoyance everything they had just desperately fought for was being given up.

As helicopter casevac was out of the question the exhausted paras fell back carrying their casualties. The SWAPO fire intensified as they regained the initiative. Mortar fire rained down on the retreating men, killing one and wounding several more including the platoon commander who CSM McAleese had to pick up and carry on his back. The urgent need to be somewhere else threatened an onset of panic; men were running blindly until halted by the CSM's determined command: "Paras don't run from terrorists!" Together with the pathfinders he managed to stop the flight, regrouped the men, and commenced an orderly withdrawal.

They moved back to the town of Cuamato and dug in for the night. Rob Gilmour's platoon was some way away from the others, and as he couldn't find anyone he knew he spent a long time sitting next to the body of the CF corporal. A tense night was spent in both sets of trenches, as everyone was aware that the next day it would all have to be done again.

In summer and winter the daytime temperatures in Angola were exceedingly hot and finding shade was a necessity, but at night in winter temperatures plummeted to near zero. The pathfinders, loaded down with a vast array of munitions, were ready for any eventuality.

At 6 o'clock in the morning the South Africans watched with satisfaction as SAAF Mirage fighter-bombers knocked out the SWAPO anti-aircraft guns while Alouette helicopter gunships pounded the SWAPO base with 20mm cannons.

C Company was picked up by Puma helicopters and deployed to another area of the enemy camp where they immediately engaged with FAPLA regulars. However, the softening-up of the position by the aircraft had made the difference and this time the enemy was more inclined to surrender. The CSM actually captured a Zairian (Congolese) officer attached to FAPLA. The drills of trench- and bunker-clearing were no less fraught with danger but this time the opposition was diminished and the South Africans were soon in complete control of the camp.

A novel feature of this operation was that it was fully covered by the press. South African Al Venter was a reporter well known to the pathfinders for his many articles on the Rhodesian war published in *Soldier of Fortune* magazine; during the second day of fighting he was in the vanguard, taking photographs during the heat of the action. Rob Gilmour, having survived the earlier close-quarter fighting, was almost killed when Venter accidentally discharged his 'souvenir' AK right next to him. Venter's subsequent article appeared in the March 1981 edition of *Scope* magazine (*see* Appendix 1). But while his text rightly concentrated on the bravery and sacrifice of the young National Servicemen, his pictures tended to show gnarled old veterans: these were of course the 'crazy foreigners'; in particular CSM McAleese.

After reorganizing and returning to base, Peter McAleese was told that he had been recommended for an award for his bravery and leadership. However, he received nothing and there was much speculation why, when his behaviour over those two days so obviously deserved recognition.

Mabalique

The third small group of pathfinders to leave Murrayhill at the end of 1980 left by vehicle with Captain Botes in charge of the next batch of candidates. One man with them was Corporal Jim Burgess who had joined the British Army in 1972, aged 15. Having served two years as a junior leader he then joined the Royal Horse Artillery in Hong Kong. He did an Ulster tour of duty and served in Belize, Cyprus and Canada. He left the British Army in 1978 and two weeks later enlisted in the Rhodesian Light Infantry, posted to 1 Commando in October where he served most of the next two years on Fireforce duties, doing nine operational para jumps, before leaving as a corporal in 1980. Prior to leaving the RLI he had successfully completed Selous Scout selection and was assured of a place in 5 Reconnaissance Commando. He was accordingly in the Culemborg Hotel, Pretoria (with Captain Gingles, later KIA with 5 Recce) awaiting transport to Phalaborwa, when Bruce Firkin, Dean Shelly and CSM McAleese came in looking for him. They told him of the new unit, bought him a load of beer, and promised lots of action. It was an easy sell as he knew nobody at 5 Recce and knew almost everyone already at 44 Parachute Brigade, including KD Clark who he had known since RLI Training Troop and had a huge amount of respect for. Next day he went to Voortrekkerhoogte and told the CO Special Forces that he wanted to go to the Pathfinders instead of 5 Recce. Corporal KD Clark, for whom Burgess had such high regard, was also on the vehicle making its way to Mabalique. KD had passed the earlier selection and was helping out with the training. A great bear of a man, he was from Fairbanks, Alaska and as an infantryman in the US Marine Corps had served three combat tours in Vietnam before joining 3 Commando, RLI where he was in constant engagement with the enemy.

Mabalique had changed subtly from the earlier visit. The Limpopo River was now in full flow with the summer rains, much to the enjoyment of the hippos wallowing in the depths, and the crocodiles, colloquially called 'flatdogs', basking in the shallows. The vegetation that was previously brown and dry was now lush and green, but hidden dangers lurked within. A rustling sound in the undergrowth was something to be avoided; it could be any number of harmless creatures or it could be a flatdog. Poisonous scorpions and snakes, particularly the black mamba, were prevalent but these old Africa hands were well experienced in taking precautions The men prepared their homes in the trenches and hovels which were

made as waterproof as possible. Then the training commenced, as physical and demanding as before. While Captain Botes retained overall supervision, actual instruction was taken by Corporal John Wessels (ex-1 Commando, RLI) and Corporal Bruce Firkin (ex-Support Commando, RLI), who drove the men every bit as hard as they had previously been driven by CSM McAleese, with the same battle drills practised day and night, over and over. The hated ammo box featured more than ever, being required on almost every run, and was the cause of much grumbling.

The qualified pathfinders gave their trainee colleagues every encouragement but were not going to give them an easy ride. Several months of inactivity had left some of them not up to the required standard of fitness, but they were well aware of this and took to the instruction with a single mindedness—to get through the training and pass selection.

As Christmas Day approached, the senior staff and some of the qualified pathfinders returned to Pretoria for leave over the holiday period. KD and Jim remained with the trainees, and Jim, using his finely honed survival skills, uplifted the boxes of army rations and traded them for beer. The resulting situation was discovered by a new arrival to the squad: Gordon Brindley, an ex-forensic scientist who had been a lieutenant in the Territorial Army, 6th Battalion, The Light Infantry, before going through RLI Training Troop and serving in 3 Commando.

A clear memory of those days remains with him:

Above: Off duty, there were no comforts to be enjoyed.

Facing left: Two English candidates settle into the harsh living and training regime at Mabalique.

When I was being kitted out in Pretoria I was issued a rail pass and travelled to Messina by train. At Messina, near the border with Zimbabwe, I was met by a Sergeant Smith who told me to jump on the Unimog and gave me a lift to Mabalique camp. After an interesting drive of a couple of hours the rain started as we entered a small camp dominated by a tin-roofed kitchen area and a green painted building which I learned later was full of crates of ammunition. The sergeant was actually part of the training team for a group of ex-Rhodesian black troops who were being recruited for 5 Recce, and was disappointed when I told him I was part of the 44 Pathfinder group and not destined for his team based in tents lower down the hill. As I got my kit off the Unimog I saw what looked like a body lying in the mud in the rain, head covered by the thin issue SADF raincoat. At the same time I was greeted by an enthusiastic pal of mine, Sean Wyatt, who had gone through basic training with me in RLI. "Who's in charge here?" I shouted and he yelled back, laughing: "He is!" pointing to a dead-drunk KD Clarke. I was taken down to a tarp-covered hooch half way down the side of the hill facing the Limpopo River, which I was to subsequently share with Sean during my time there. At night you could hear the drums beating across the river as if you were on some kind of Rider Haggard film set with frogs croaking and insects clicking away. The most amazing thing was the rise and fall in the level of the river, depending on the rainstorms many miles away upriver. Sometimes the water could be seen quickly rising and covering the track next to the river, and two days later the water was low enough for Zimbabweans to walk across the river into South Africa.

The culture of the camp was somewhat eccentric to say the least. We were only about 15 men but we had mountains of Ouma rusks and Ready Maid orange juice stacked everywhere. The green brick building was crammed full of crates of rifle ammo and grenades and mortar bombs with some of the lads sleeping among the crates. Beer was jammed into a large paraffin-powered fridge. Our main enemy was boredom but we certainly improvised. Apart from trying to clear the fridge of beer every day we played Risk; we also had a dartboard, which we eventually shot up with our rifles. We were very lucky since some of the lads were still in the kitchen area behind the board and yet were not hit. Another time, Dave Barr was demonstrating the operation of the South African grenades to another trainee and was happily throwing them down the hill near our hooch. The camp water pipe was shredded, as was the tarpaulin that formed our roof.

Gordon also remembered playing chicken one day with his old Canadian friend Sean, rolling M26 grenades ten metres or so away and seeing who was the last to hit the ground before they went off. This adult version of *Lord of the Flies* came to an end when the instructors returned and the serious business of hard training resumed.

Living in these simple surroundings without the distractions of modern society, it was possible for some things to take on an importance out of place in the normal world. The board game Risk became an important part of off-duty entertainment. It is a game of world domination where alliances are formed and, when necessary, allies were stabbed in the back in order to gain advantage: only a board game, but friendships got strained and bitter disputes ensued. Gunplay was resorted to on only one occasion but it did lead to a period of tense anticipation.

Pete Morpuss and Dave Barr used to feed a duiker which visited their hooch, but this pleasant pastime was put in jeopardy when KD found out, determined to get the small deer into the cooking pot. He was happy for them to feed it up first, but Pete and Dave made sure he never got around to killing it.

Englishman Mark Sullivan reflects on his earlier military career in the French Foreign Legion and the Rhodesian Armoured Car Regiment. He has on one side his R4 rifle, and resting on the other side are ex-Rhodesian folding-butt FN rifles in their usual camouflage paint. These were used during physical training.

The stock of tinned rations was all well and good but the lack of fresh food was being felt until Captain Botes shot three roaming feral cows, still called *mombes* by the ex-Rhodesians. With the greatest of difficulty the carcasses were manhandled onto a truck and taken to Mabalique where Alan Cauvin set about skinning, gutting and preparing them. Alan was a Rhodesian farm boy who had served in the Rhodesian African Rifles, and after a few drinks he would break into 'Sweet Banana' or any number of their regimental songs. Singlehandedly he butchered the first beast, then the second, both strung up in the branch of a tree. After finishing the second animal he was exhausted and suggested a Brit do the last one. Jim, bribed by the promise of alcohol, took up the challenge and managed to produce a bloody, shredded thing, which was considered okay for a first attempt. The two good carcasses where driven to a nearby rural store and exchanged for fresh vegetables, while the shredded remains of a once-noble beast provided meat for the camp for some time to come.

Captain Botes' duties took him elsewhere, leaving the camp under the senior NCO, Sergeant Graham Gillmore. Gordon Brindley had discovered marula trees in the area; these trees produced a fruit much loved by elephants which had such a long digestive process that the fruit fermented in their stomachs, leaving the creatures drunk. Harvesting the fruit became a popular pastime. Yeast, water and watermelon were added; the fruit was then pulped and left to ferment. Obviously, the longer it was left the stronger the brew became but such was the lack of alternative leisure interests that the immature concoction was consumed within days by impatient and thirsty soldiers.

Left: An early experimental brew of fermented marula juice. Once Gordon Brindley had perfected the technique far larger quantities were produced but never enough to meet the demand.

With the training nearly over plans were made to move the squad back to Murrayhill and then to the Drakensberg for the selection test phase. Wessels and Firkin suggested that an end-of-training party should be held on the final night before departure; they had saved an amount of tracer rounds, para-illumination mortar rounds and flares for the purpose of celebration. Earlier they had seen a demonstration of how military parties were carried out by a spectacular night-time light show put on by the army camp in Venda, far off to the west. Well, the pathfinders would do better.

Official word had gone round the camp to be aware that the Zimbabwean police would be carrying out an anti-stock theft deployment just over the Limpopo in Zimbabwe, but to the pathfinders this was not something to be overly concerned about as the pathfinder training would not affect matters over there. While these men had given total commitment and loyal service to Rhodesia, they had lost the war and seen the country embrace Marxism. There was sympathy for the whites, and those few blacks who hadn't voted for Mugabe, whose circumstances did not allow them to leave, but as hard as it was they were now a potential enemy country.

Come the party, come the drinking and high spirits. The night-time sky was lit up by illumination flares gently floating down beneath small parachutes creating ghostly grey shadows on the ground; R4 magazines were loaded with tracer rounds and individuals practised writing their names among the stars. Bang! Off went the mortar, firing para-illumination rounds. And again. And again, then *whoomp*! A high-explosive (HE) blast not far away caused some interest; more para-illumination rounds go up, then another high-explosive blast. It must be remembered that these men carried out live-firing battle drills almost every day, and during mock camp attacks the mortar was used to drop HE rounds close to the assaulting troops, so the bangs and crashes of the party were not something to cause them alarm. But that was not the case with more sensitive souls not far away.

Next morning, the camp was cleaned up and the damaged water pipe peppered with HE shrapnel was repaired yet again, the same pipe that ran from the kitchen via a pump down the bank to the river: the only source of water for the camp. As soon as everything was in good order a lorry carrying the selection squad set off for Murrayhill, while Sergeant Gillmore waited with some of the qualified men for the agreed departure time of 12 o'clock midday. An unknown vehicle then pulled up into the camp, which was so out of the way that nobody just happened to 'drop in'.

An officer got out, with two questions: "Who's in charge here?" and "What happened last night?"

The Zimbabwean police must have been closer than anyone in the camp realized because they thought that they were under attack and immediately reported the matter to Harare. Comrade Mugabe of course wasted no time in protesting to the government in Pretoria who were stumped for an explanation. Questions filtered down the chain of command, resulting in the arrival of this rather concerned officer, who received the simple and honest answer: "We are the Pathfinder Company, 44 Para Brigade and we had a party."

Some weeks later, a Board of Inquiry was held into the circumstances of this incident, and the key personnel in camp that night were called to give evidence before a committee chaired by Colonel Breytenbach. Nothing came of it ... of course.

Chapter 3
Camp at Murrayhill

Peacetime soldiering

New officers had arrived in the company: Captain Graham Peak, ex-Rhodesian, and Lieutenant Fred Verduin, an American who after service in the US Infantry was commissioned in the Rhodesian Grey's Scouts before moving to South Africa.

Time spent at Murrayhill was not productive for the pathfinders. Often there would be a need for a trip into Pretoria, maybe to go to the bank, or dentist or any number of other excuses. Maybe another new arrival from abroad was to be met, but invariably it resulted in a lunchtime pint in the Culemborg Hotel, which invariably led to an afternoon drinking session.

The SADF was essentially a peacetime army where duty on the border was an occasional, often unwanted, requirement, but the pathfinders were itching to fight and defeat the terrorist threat, which in southern Africa took the form of black 'freedom fighters'. In order to achieve that aim the pathfinders were happy to fight along side other black troops, and to engage white opponents, be they Soviet, East German or Cuban, so there was no clear-cut racial motive to their presence in the SADF. But they did want to be fighting and not sitting twiddling their thumbs in camp. Ex-Scots Guardsman Colin Brown was a qualified pathfinder but was doing duty in the kitchen when he experienced something of the cultural differences:

The only solid structures at the Murrayhill camp were the old original houses and barns of the broken-down farm.

FAPLA

The armed wing of the MPLA (*Movimento Popular de Libertação de Angola*, the Popular Movement for the Liberation of Angola) was originally called EPLA (*Ejercito Popular de Liberación de Angola*) in the early 1960s during its revolutionary uprising against the Portuguese colonists. After the left-wing military coup in Portugal in 1974 and the announcement by the new government to pull out of Angola, the EPLA changed its name to FAPLA (*Forças Armadas Populares de Libertação de Angola*, the People's Armed Forces for the Liberation of Angola). This new force, with Soviet weapons and training backing it, was organized on conventional military lines, with aircraft and heavy weapons such as tanks and artillery.

Soviet surrogates in the form of the Cuban army and air force, together with FAPLA, eventually destroyed the pro-Western FNLA (*Frente Nacional para a Libertação de Angola*, the National Front for the Liberation of Angola), led by Holden Roberto, and all but drove Jonas Savimbi's UNITA from the country. Agostinho Neto's MPLA took control of the government and FAPLA became *de facto* the Angolan Army. Having been conceived as a guerrilla movement, FAPLA now found itself in a conventional military role engaged in counter-insurgency operations against UNITA guerrillas, operating from the eastern border areas of Angola and Zambia. Constant training and vigilance by Cuban and Soviet advisors and instructors ensured that FAPLA, although never up to the standards of modern Western armies, was by an African yardstick at least, a force to be reckoned with.

One morning we looked outside after breakfast to see one of the black pan-divers [a washing-up fatigue] just gazing into space. Come suppertime he was still sat there; another worker said that a witchdoctor had put a curse on him. It turned out that he had had an argument with one of the other pan-divers, who had gone into Hammanskraal and paid a witchdoctor to put a curse on him.

The next morning we woke to find him still in the same place gazing into space, having not moved at all since the previous day. The black who had put the curse on him started to look worried and mumbled that he had not thought the victim would take it so seriously, but we would need to get another witchdoctor to remove the curse. Of course he didn't have enough money and asked for help. As we were only paid R275 a month we were not exactly rich but we chipped in to sort this guy out, as he was a decent lad who worked hard and was a good laugh.

Later the 'new' witchdoctor appeared and went through his repertoire of removing the curse; we watched with mild amusement as a chance of a story in the bar that night. The witchdoctor did his stuff, dancing about and throwing potions and dust on the victim's head and after about 30 minutes he declared the spell lifted. He then asked who had put the curse on the man in the first place, and when he was told we watched his face drop with him leaving in haste, saying that the spell could not be removed by anyone but the original witchdoctor because he was more powerful. This caused uproar among the staff and the victim again fell back into his coma.

On the third day the guy was still sat in the same place gazing into space. All the locals explained that there was nothing that they could do; they had gone to see the original witchdoctor to ask for the

This house was first given to the Pathfinder Company's senior NCO ranks to use, but with the company more or less permanently deployed in the operational area, the other ranks took possession of it.

curse to be removed. He had demanded an exorbitant sum to remove the spell, which of course they could not pay. Rather than upset the witchdoctor, they all filed out of his hut and went home. The next day we heard a commotion and behind the kitchen we saw the staff carrying away the poor man's body on their shoulders, trooping off into the bush in the direction of Hammanskraal.

As well as the camp being nothing like a real barracks, the stores and equipment were not controlled in a normal army fashion either. Weapons consisted of every type of stolen, captured and regular-issue item, to which the pathfinders had complete and unregulated access. Without any paperwork or training pamphlets Sergeant Gillmore taught himself; then gave instruction on the unfamiliar HF and VHF radio equipment.

WOII George Kay was another arrival at Murrayhill. While in his mind he wanted to be with the combat troops, his advanced years dictated that his role was going to be that of camp admin, and despite his best efforts, progress was slow. George's happiest moments were when the pathfinders were in camp and he could regale them with his latest plan to take the war to the enemy, something he had been doing since he parachuted into Arnhem during the Second World War.

The pathfinders maintained some terms and expressions used widely in the Rhodesian Army: an enemy soldier or terrorist was 'a gook'—the Americanism from Vietnam days. To kill the enemy was to 'slot floppies' (from their tendency to flop over when shot), food was called 'graze', and a black woman was 'a nanny'. Another old habit some were unable to break was the smoking of *dagga*, or marijuana, and although it was considered totally inappropriate for a man on duty to be under the influence, to occasionally mellow out in leisure time was quite acceptable. Dope though was not the cause of most of their problems: a soldier's ability to drink to excess is

Jim Burgess, Paul Whitehead and Kiwi Watson.

Sergeant Art Nulty and Mark Griffiths. Nulty was a British ex-RLI medic with a passion for weapons and gadgets; he kept everyone amused with his latest gizmo development.

universal, and these were hardened soldiers who for years had lived for today because tomorrow they might be dead.

The bilingual nature of South Africa had bypassed some regions of the country. For instance, it was possible in Natal to find people who spoke no Afrikaans at all, and in the Transvaal there were Afrikaners who didn't speak any English whatsoever. The army was totally Afrikaner-dominated and contained men who insisted in speaking only Afrikaans to the foreigners, so divisions were bound to develop. At Murrayhill the South Africans would announce a *braai*, a social event where everyone should enjoy a barbequed meal, a few drinks, and polite conversation. Not so the *uitlanders*; it was an occasion to get drunk, eat burnt food and tell the South Africans what they were doing wrong in the army.

Lieutenant Fred Verduin served as an enlisted man in the US Infantry before going to Rhodesia where he joined the Grey's Scouts, the mounted infantry unit; there he passed a potential officers' course and was promoted to second lieutenant. He joined the SADF as a full lieutenant.

On one such evening Jim Burgess, known for being the first at the drink, was in conversation with a young South African he hadn't seen before, and having put him right on a few things, told him in no uncertain terms what he thought of him personally. On parade next morning the pathfinders were introduced to a new South African engineer officer who was joining the company: Lieutenant Brown and Jim's drinking buddy from the night before. It was announced that Captain Botes was leaving the army and the new OC of the Pathfinder Company was Captain Dries Velthuizen.

Another new arrival at the brigade was Major Alastair MacKenzie, a New Zealander who had served in the Kiwi army from 1966 until 1973, including a tour in Vietnam as platoon commander where he was Mentioned in Dispatches. In 1973 he switched to the British Army and joined the Parachute Regiment, serving in 3 Para as 2IC Patrol Company and Battalion Training Officer. He then passed selection and spent four years in 22SAS Regiment before leaving in 1980 to join 44 Parachute Brigade as 2IC Operations and Training. As part of his introduction to the SADF the major was taken by Colonel Breytenbach to the workshops of the Council for Scientific and Industrial Research (CSIR) in Pretoria where he was shown the production line of the Ratel armoured fighting vehicle. Pointing out the square metal grill bolted to the rear, the colonel asked MacKenzie what he thought it was.

"An aerial? RPG deflector?" the major replied.

"No," the colonel said, "it's a *braaivleis* ... the barbeque. Welcome to bush soldiering!"

On 2 February 1981 Major MacKenzie presented a paper laying out his assessment of Pathfinder Company:

General

1. The Pathfinder Company of 44 Para Bde is currently being employed as a recce unit in Sector 10 under operational command of the sector commander. Other tasks have been carried out by the unit on a one-off basis.

2. The company is composed mainly of non-South Africans who have generally come from Rhodesia, having worked with the military in that country.

3. There are currently 23 operational members of the company with another 11 on selection/ continuation training. A nominal roll is attached at Annex A.

4. The company is based at Murrayhill with HQ 44 Para Bde.

5. The members are not happy and with, I believe, good reasons and it is essential that the complete pathfinder concept is reviewed otherwise current members of the company will resign and recruiting will cease.

Operations

6. The company has formed an efficient, aggressive unit and has gained a good reputation for effectiveness in its operations. However, the skills of members of the company are limited in other specialized fields, e.g. vehicle operations. Members of the company have few individual skills of a standard sufficient for small-group operations, e.g. medic, signal and demolition. Currently a training team is being formed; unfortunately this team is composed of some personnel who failed pathfinder selection and few who have specialist skills themselves. These instructors will therefore need to be instructed themselves. This is not a satisfactory situation.

7. It is essential that all members of the company must have good individual skills training in the near future, enabling the company to increase its expertise and, more importantly, its employability. More one-off ops must not be accepted until sufficient training has been carried out to the satisfaction of the Pathfinder Officer Commanding.

8. At the completion of any operation in which pathfinders participate a complete debrief must be carried out by a member of the intelligence staff. This enables much value to be gained and also ensures the unit is always improving.

Training

9. The company has a high standard of minor tactics but a distinct weakness in specialist courses. Members of the company must be sent on specialist courses at established training schools or units to ensure that the highest standard of instruction is received from an experienced instructor on the subject involved. Each patrol of five or six men must have the following trained personnel:

   - patrol commander
   - signaller (training to 12 wpm minimum)
   - Medic (medical training to include a minimum of four weeks in a civilian hospital, casualty department)
   - demolitionist
   - linguist/photographer

10. If different operations are being planned then a build-up of other, but not so vital, skill must be achieved, e.g. astro-navigation, languages etc.

Organization

11. At the moment the company is a conglomerate of small groups operating or training in different areas with no patrol/stick structure. Members of each patrol work with other patrols on a very ad-hoc basis. This does not enable an *esprit de corps* to build up nor does it enable patrols to build up their group skills and abilities. Whenever possible patrols must be composed of the same personnel for operation and training and their programme must be planned accordingly.

12. The organization of the Pathfinder Company is laid down clearly in '44 Para Bde Pathfinder Ops Provisional'. If the company is to operate efficiently then the organization must be formed and adhered to.

13. There are no 'A' or 'Q' [Admin or Quartermaster] staff with the Pathfinders and this is a disturbing deficiency. To carry out operations efficiently a unit must have an efficient 'A' and 'Q' backup—it does not have to be perfect but at the moment it does not exist at all.

Promotion

14. Promotion for NCOs in the SADF is controlled by CSP. Non-South African personnel, particularly Rhodesians, are given a rank on arrival appropriate to their qualifications. Non-South African NCOs cannot be promoted until they have completed 12 months' service. However, there are troopers

Top and left: The convoy of light fighting vehicles arrived at Murrayhill to be fitted with weapons and radios.

Left: Ex-US Marine drill instructor KD Clark confirms that the smoke discharger is working. The highway interchange exit for the Murrayhill camp was used as a first test bed. One vehicle produced smoke that completely covered the four-lane highway and stopped all traffic for several minutes. This was not condoned by the colonel, but provided a dramatic example of what the system was capable of.

Left: Col Breytenbach and the pathfinder convoy ready to move.

and NCOs within the Pathfinder Company who merit promotion within a year. A system should be introduced into contracts for non-South Africans enabling them to be promoted, or demoted, before they have completed their 12 months. Obviously any rank changes must be substantiated by relevant documentation.

Coming from outside the unit, and considering his impressive background, the opinion of Major MacKenzie was valued by the pathfinders, especially the conclusion to his assessment that they were "well motivated, dedicated and well able to carry out their recce role on the border". However, Colonel Breytenbach had been up to his usual secret planning and all talk of training and reorganization came to a halt when WOII Frank Green appeared with his latest project—a convoy of light fighting vehicles.

Sabre vehicles

Sergeants Penrose and Dean Evans had enlarged WOII Green's team; they produced nine vehicles to take the colonel and the pathfinders terrorist-hunting. Again these vehicles were 'acquired' and converted in the CSIR workshops. The convoy consisted of three Toyota Land Cruisers, two mounting .50 calibre Browning machine guns and one for WOII Green's own use, armed with a 20mm Husqvarna cannon scrounged from the South African Air Force. Three three-quarter-ton Land Rovers carried twin 7.62mm FN MAG general-purpose machine guns mounted at the rear, each with a 500-round box welded to the side of the pedestal, plus a single machine gun for the commander.

Captain Graham Peak and Company Sergeant-Major Peter McAleese.

Three 2.5-ton Mercedes Unimog trucks were to carry the fuel, rations and ammunition needed for long-range patrols behind enemy lines, also fitted with a machine gun for the commander. All vehicles were camouflage-painted which, with their belligerent design, set them apart from all other brown-painted SADF vehicles.

All the bodywork was removed and the chassis strengthened by welding and bolting alloy bars in front under the seats. Duplicate fuel tanks were added behind the original ones and all were packed with multi-mesh aluminium to deter fuel explosions from incendiary-round strikes. The self-sealing tyres were foam-filled to counter bullet holes or the ever-likely thorn punctures, and two spare tyres were carried. A protective mesh grill was placed over the engine compartment, and testing showed that this grill needed a canvas screen under it to prevent veld grass seeds clogging the air intakes. The gun platform was a solid tray of three-quarter-inch steel fixed over the rear axle. There were no doors or windscreens; instead a front-expanded mesh grill protected the driver and commander, and boxes for radios were situated between them. Short-range VHF sets were used for inter-vehicle communication and HF sets for the long distance link back to base. Storage bins were set behind the driver and commander, and jerry cans for water and fuel were clamped to a quick-release device on the rear and sides of the vehicle. If the cans were ignited by a hit the No. 2 on the gun could pull a lever and they would fall away.

Travelling west then north the convoy crossed the Kalahari Desert, perfecting their fighting formations and battle drills en route.

Knowing the difficult type of terrain they were preparing for, each Sabre vehicle had a winch to pull itself or another vehicle out of soft sand, boggy vlei or washed-away roads. Another extra was its smoke dispenser, based on the Soviet armoured vehicle smoke-generating method. A small container of brake fluid was placed over the exhaust manifold with a valve connected to a tap on the dashboard; when the tap was opened the fluid dropped onto the manifold producing dense clouds of white smoke from the exhaust pipe. This system enabled each vehicle to lay down a screen for self-protection or to cover the manoeuvres of others.

The embroidered arm badge worn by Sector 10 personnel.

The convoy only arrived at Murrayhill two days before the company was due to set off for the border, so with time pressing crews were assigned their vehicles and familiarization commenced. Drivers developed maintenance routines; signallers brushed up their antenna theory, and everyone learned to strip, clean, and fire the .50 calibre Browning machine guns which only a few had handled before. One man with vast experience with the weapons was Corporal Dave Barr who was given the responsibility of maintaining and instructing on the guns. These particular weapons were of the latest model where the head spacing did not need to be set; the barrels were screwed fully in then unscrewed two full turns. It was noticed that they didn't have serial numbers.

In 1969, at the age of 17, Dave began his military career with the US Marine Corps, receiving 57 air medals while serving on a helicopter gunship in Vietnam. He left the Marines in 1972, but felt the need to seek adventure and another cause. He chose to serve five years in the Israeli paras, and later in the RLI, and finally in South Africa.

One of the Toyota Land Cruisers was picked as the colonel's command vehicle with Sergeant Gillmore as signaller, Dave Barr as gunner, and Lang Price as driver. Lang was another American from the RLI, but one with a solid military-academy education.

Personal preparations did not take long; everyone's next of kin details were already held in the brigade office but a note was added that families should only be informed of death, as nobody wanted their loved ones unnecessarily worried by injuries when it would not be possible for them to make contact in the operational area. Subsequent events showed that this request was ignored, and notices were sent.

The men had little or nothing in the way of personal belongings so it was easy to pack their few civilian clothes into a suitcase which remained at Murrayhill. One extra item that each man required because of his exposed position on the Sabres was goggles, as a precaution against wind, rain and dust. After much hunting in Pretoria and surrounding areas a number of ski masks were bought, the gaudy-coloured elastic straps dulled down with felt-tipped marker pens.

Vehicles were packed and then with the colonel's Sabre in front the company headed west from Pretoria. Almost immediately one after another started to break down. The fuel used to fill the petrol tanks had been taken from old oil drums cleaned out by Dave Barr, but as it transpired, they had not been fully drained of water so the fuel was contaminated causing the filters to block. A problem that was easy to cure but it did not make for an auspicious start to the adventure.

It was intended to take a slow two-week trip to Sector 10 to allow the crews to familiarize themselves with the nature and workings of the vehicles, and to develop the tactics they might expect to use on deep-penetration patrols.

An operational area base camp. Many infantry companies carried out tours of duty on the border, based at such camps, from where they patrolled their area of responsibility. Conditions were very basic but slightly more consideration was given to Citizen Force personnel than the poor, ever-suffering National Servicemen.

The route took them through the northern Karoo then up into South West Africa where, keeping to the eastern side of the country, they drove along the border with Botswana marked by a dirt road and game fence. Once into this unpopulated region they could then set about the job of practising their battle drills.

Two-vehicle sections were formed; the commander in a Land Cruiser and his second-in-command in a Land Rover, thus giving a good mix of firepower. In open country tactical movement formations were practised, where invariably the colonel would be in the lead; this arrangement would remain in place throughout their active service. Routines for laagering at night were developed, as were ambush and anti-ambush procedures.

Night-driving without lights was practised using head-mounted image intensifiers—with mixed results. Because the image seen by the driver was only two dimensional it made judging distance so difficult that on a moonlit night it was sometimes better without them.

Live firing took place during this phase of the move as they rehearsed anti-ambush drills. The Sabres were dripping with weapons of war. Every vehicle carried a similar payload: the main armourment mounted in position plus an enormous amount of ammunition in storage bins, an RPG-7 anti-tank rocket launcher and rockets, an M79 (blooper) grenade launcher, and claymore mines for camp defence. Each member of the crew had his R4 rifle and either his own personal pistol or the issue Star 9mm pistol known to the pathfinders as a 'bush hammer' because it was so unreliable. The belts of .50-cal ammunition were hand-linked to provide a mix of ball, tracer and armour-piercing rounds.

One evening Lang and Dave were refuelling the command vehicle from jerry cans while Sergeant Gillmore brewed up some tea about five yards away, when sun-warmed petrol fumes seeped over the ground toward the gas cooker. Then *whoosh*! Up in flames went the whole back of the vehicle with Lang and Dave in the middle. The colonel immediately yelled a command: "Get that vehicle out of here." So Dave jumped into the front of the vehicle, started it up and sped away to get out of the laager and away from the other vehicles; Lang had succeeded in freeing the fire extinguisher and was running behind dousing the flames, which he managed before any noticeable damage was done.

Individual equipment was the ordinary issue Pattern 1970 webbing of belt, yoke and ammo pouches but this was designed for the R1 rifles so could not take the 35-round R4 magazines. Brown nylon Para-Fox chest webbing took the pistol, grenades and six spare rifle magazines; each man had two 50-round R4 magazines protruding from the magazine pouches. Spare clothing and personal items would normally be carried in the large webbing pack but because of the extra needs of these specialist troops Colonel Breytenbach had bought butterfly-framed rucksacks for his men at unit expense. With such a load of ammunition and petrol there was concern about the ever-present danger of landmines. Other military off-road vehicles like the V-hulled Buffel were specially designed to protect the troops inside in the event of a mine detonation, and this was successfully achieved by deflecting the blast up the armoured sides of the vehicle. Because the Sabres were light unarmoured attack vehicles it was hoped that by staying off the roads this would lessen the risk.

The journey continued, taking in the sandy expanse of the Kalahari Desert. The approaching winter meant that the temperature dropped significantly at night as the pathfinders bedded down on the ground next to the vehicles in laager. The beauty of the landscape was not lost on them, and they took satisfaction that adventure holidaymakers paid good money for a similar experience. Herds of springbok and impala could be seen in the early morning.

A vital piece of personal kit was a camera, and many striking photographs were taken of fiery red sunsets and scenic views, usually including a Sabre because there was no doubt that they really looked the part. In the evening Sergeant Gillmore tuned a radio into various news stations: the English service of Radio Moscow with is outrageous propaganda was always good for a laugh, the Voice of America was better, but for accurate news of local events the Africa Service of the BBC World Service was the most trusted.

The ration pack was designed with young National Servicemen in mind, consisting as it did of sweetened fruit, sweetened drinks and sweets—plenty of them. Consequently CSM McAleese introduced the men to his bush recipe for the perfect end to a day dining experience: empty into a mess tin whatever cans of meat were to hand, add peas, fruit, cheese, and anything else that no one wanted. Stir in a generous amount of curry powder and as much piri piri sauce as was allowed by the Geneva Convention. Once eaten, never forgotten. One particular brew stripped the paint off the steel helmet it was cooked in, but it was nevertheless eaten, paint and all. While in the bush during this move and on all operational deployments waste was buried in a hole and before moving off, the area was cleared of anything that might leave spoor or provide intelligence to the enemy.

Above and facing page: The Pathfinder Company parade with their vehicles to be blessed by the *dominee*, the ubiquitous priest found in all SADF units.

Left: A shield painted by Mark Griffiths depicting the various parachute qualification badges held by members of the unit. Above is the Parabat beret badge and below is the internationally recognized symbol of the pathfinders, a flaming torch. The central emblem with the stylized 44 is based on the German infantry combat badge.

In their new home the pathfinders' vehicles created much interest and envy.

Colonel Breytenbach took the pathfinders northward, following the back ways along the eastern border to Gobabis and from there into Bushmanland; then on to Okavango and Oshivelo. This fleeting brush with South West African society introduced the men to the still-prevalent German culture, which with the Afrikaans influence reinforced even more the pathfinders' *uitlander* status. Roads were untarred and because of the very real landmine threat the colonel took them overland whenever possible. In earlier times the survival of the Dutch Voortrekkers and German-speaking pioneer settlers depended entirely on their self-reliance; it was up to them to rise above every hardship that a barren, hostile country threw at them. They did so and it bred into their descendants a strongly confident (some might say overbearing) character. As the pathfinders progressed on their journey north the red soil of South Africa changed to the yellow sand of the Kalahari, which in turn became the white dust of Owamboland. Their self-reliance was tested to the full as problems arose, be they mechanical breakdown, vehicles sunk up to the axles in drifting sand or an impossible river crossing. They would stand back, scratch their heads, roll up their sleeves and set about the task in hand.

The journey was unfortunately not without incident as a long-held animosity between CSM McAleese and WOII Green turned into a vicious altercation. WOII Frank Green whose love of producing killing machines no matter how indiscriminate, had earned himself the nickname of 'Genocide Frank'. And CSM Peter McAleese's burning sense of right and wrong had led him to violence before. Away from the company the two men faced off and came to blows, resulting in WOII Green's face becoming severely battered and bruised, and CSM McAleese being relieved of his appointment and sent back to Murrayhill.

Chapter 4
Operations begin

South West Africa

The convoy eventually reached the camp at Okotopi to the great relief of the several pathfinders still stationed there who had ideas that they had been abandoned. It did not take long for the new arrivals to discover the delights of their new home: there were very few, in fact none. As well as the miserable standard of the two meals a day, mostly rice and meat bones, they found there was no tea option which they had enjoyed at Murrayhill. Only chicory coffee was supplied which had to be the worst-tasting hot drink ever invented. Then there were the fly-infested horse lines, and the dreaded toilets.

WOII Dennis Croukamp was appointed company sergeant-major, and while he was superbly qualified and well deserving of the position, the circumstances requiring it left a dark cloud over the company. Colonel Breytenbach, confident that he had a unit absolutely primed for active service, approached Sector 10 headquarters with the aim of finding work for his men.

One puzzling activity in the camp did take their interest, the 'mad minute'. Every once in a while it would be announced that in the evening there would be a 'mad minute', so at last light everyone in camp went to the perimeter wall and waited for the signal to open fire. Once given everyone blazed away to their front with whatever they had to shoot with for the allotted minute, then silence, and everyone returned to their tents for weapon cleaning. What this

The Buffel

The Buffel (buffalo) was first introduced in 1978, due to an escalation in the number of landmine incidents on the border; there were 327 alone in 1980, almost one a day. The army required a vehicle that was both anti-tank-mine-resistant and armoured against small-arms fire, including rocket-propelled grenades. The Buffel was widely used as an infantry personnel carrier, and for vehicle patrols in combat and non-combat roles. It was built on the undercarriage of a Mercedes 2.5 Unimog truck, with a V-shaped, armoured, ten-passenger bay, and a small enclosed armoured compartment for the driver. The high centre of gravity made for a bumpy ride, but the height of the vehicle was good for observation into the passing bush. Debussing was made simple by dropping the sides.

Early morning, heading north across the 'cut line', the fence that marked the border between South West Africa and Angola.

Top: Colonel Breytenbach plans his route with an officer from 32 Battalion. Dave Barr sits behind his .50-calibre Browning machine gun; the author Sergeant Gillmore stands at right.

had to do with a sound defence strategy was lost on the pathfinders, but being guests they felt obliged to throw their full energy into supporting the activity.

British regiments had a padre to supply the religious needs of the men; he was normally a man of character who was sparing in his criticism of the soldiery because of their special circumstances. Within the SADF a *dominee* was an all-powerful figure who was answerable to no one in camp. He preserved the overpowering influence held by the staunchly Protestant Dutch Reformed Church in South African society, and was the first point of contact for any National Serviceman who had a problem. The members of the Pathfinder Company apparently presented a challenge for the dominee, and a number of them at various locations tried to engage with the men; they were always treated with respect but for some reason went away with the impression that these foreigners were ungodly heathens. The name 'Philistines' thus came to be associated with the unit.

The pathfinders set about the task of fine-tuning their weapons and vehicles. Firing ranges were set up and sights were zeroed in, and the men who were already on the border took their place within the vehicle crews. WOII Green found it impossible to get the 20mm cannon firing correctly so after much disappointment it was exchanged for a .50 cal Browning from Koevoet, the South African Police anti-terrorist unit. All of this took time but the men set to it with a purpose. Until the Pathfinder Company became better known there was often some confusion when the vehicles pulled into a camp to refuel. The puzzled National Serviceman on duty would stand, clipboard in hand looking for a non-existent registration plate.

"You can't fill up here," he would say.

"Operational vehicle," the pathfinders would say and fill up anyway, leaving the clerk to worry about his paperwork.

Lieutenant Verduin arranged for the dominee to bless the guns, and a parade was arranged for the ceremony with the vehicles lined up and the troops in front. While it seemed a strange thing to the non-British element, it was a long-held tradition in the Royal Artillery.

Then on 12 April the company received a warning order to move, and the colonel called the men together for a briefing. Vehicles were taken out to a range area for the weapons to be zeroed in, but on their return to camp they

Centre: A patrol from 32 Battalion, with its own distinctive camouflage uniform. The battalion included several ex-RLI colleagues, and it was always a pleasure for the pathfinders to work with these hardened combat veterans.

Right: On the pathfinders' first camp attack only the anti-aircraft machine gunners stayed to fight. This position consisted of three 14.5 guns which were taken back to South West Africa. The company retained one for its own use; a second went to airfield defence and the third, a non-firing one, was put in a children's playground.

This SWAPO machine gunner was wounded in the leg and, unable to run, chose to shoot himself in the head on the approach of the pathfinder Sabres.

Weapon familiarization and sight-zeroing took place on makeshift ranges. Experience in the Rhodesian bush war showed that the FN MAG general-purpose machine gun was more often fired from the hip or shoulder than in the prone position for which it was designed. The Land Rover-mounted twin machine guns were likewise tested in an awesome display of firepower.

were told the op had been cancelled. The next day it was on again, and consisted of a simple task of deploying a recce team from 32 Battalion some 45 miles into Angola.

The company moved first to Ondangwa, then at midnight farther north to another of those company base camps at Okolongo where they collected the well-known and respected Captain Willem Ratte and his recce team. One of the 32 Battalion NCOs was Robert Clifford from the British Virgin Islands, and an old colleague from Support Commando, RLI. He had been one of the very first to move south.

Early next morning they moved over the 'cut line', the fence that marked the border, and into Angola with Captain Ratte navigating. Wrapped up against the cold air but alert to danger there suddenly appeared a man on a bicycle in front of the command Sabre

"He's got a rifle," barked the colonel as the man swerved into thick bush.

Immediately Lang Price hit the brakes and Dave Barr opened up with his beloved .50 cal, while the colonel joined in with the front-mounted general-purpose machine gun. At the same time Sergeant Gillmore dismounted the vehicle and commenced firing his R4 into the bush into which the cyclist had disappeared.

The following vehicles came up into a firing line and not knowing what the target was commenced firing in the same direction as the command vehicle. After several thousand rands' worth of munitions had been expended the colonel called, "Cease fire!" Gordon Brindley had a worrying experience during this exchange:

Top: Gordon Brindley and Steve Bertrand.

Above: The company foot-patrolling in Angola find convenient signs to prove it.

> Mike Landskov was the gunner and I was number two. We'd worked out a gun drill for reloading the gun during action. The feedbox was on the left of the gun so on 'action right' I merely stood left forward on the back of the vehicle as the gun swung to face the threat. On 'action left' I was to leap off the moving vehicle (if the gun barrel didn't knock me off first) holding a full box of .50 ammo (about 35kg), run around the back and climb back on board where I could

Top: Pete Morpuss's Land Rover suffered considerably from mechanical problems to Peter's frustration and the colonel's anger. It broke its back at one point, causing the rear end to be higher than the front; the amusing result was likened to the jalopy in the Beverly Hillbillies.

Centre: Captain Peak's all-Rhodesian Land Cruiser crew.

Above: Lieutenant Verduin and KD Clark pose, while Mac McEwen doesn't. Mac served in the Prince of Wales's Own Regiment of Yorkshire before joining 3 Commando, RLI.

service the gun. It sounds stupid now since I can't remember the need to leap off the vehicle at all. When the shots rang out we were at 'action left'. I did the drill correctly and leaped off the vehicle and to my horror saw the Toyota Sabre accelerate away from me, I ran like hell with a box of ammo in my arms swearing as my lack of breath would allow. It must have been a strange sight since I was wearing my para helmet (for low branches) and remember my brown plastic raincoat flapping around like a flag. When I got to the moving vehicle found I couldn't climb up with the heavy box. The only result of this silly experience was for the tiffies [mechanics] at Oshakati to weld a metal footrest on the back of the vehicle to allow me to climb up in a future situation. I think we changed the drill after that.

A sweep line was formed to check the contact area, but no body was found; only a battered rifle magazine containing 7.62mm NATO rounds. On thinking about what he had seen the colonel said, "It was a G3 rifle so he was probably UNITA. He'll have a story to tell when he gets home."

The radio rod antennas fitted to the Sabres did not have the range to carry back to base, so every two hours the convoy stopped in all-round defence so that Sergeant Gillmore could throw up a slopping-wire diapole antenna to make his scheduled radio call. Gilly had started his military service in the Territorial Army, Royal Engineers. Deciding in 1973 on a full-time career he joined the Grenadier Guards where he experienced mechanized infantry in West Germany, tours in Ulster and the inevitable ceremonial duties in London, He was a member of their successful shooting team for two years before leaving in 1977 to join the Rhodesian Light Infantry. Promotion came fast and Gilly went from trooper to sergeant in two years, and spent the following six months as Signals Troop Sergeant. Gilly left the army with the majority of the foreigners on 30 April 1980 as he had already applied, and

Colonel Breytenbach's command Land Cruiser was invariably the lead vehicle in the convoy. Lang Price was the driver, Dave Barr the gunner and Sergeant Graham Gillmore the company signaller.

had been accepted, into the SADF. On getting word from his old comrades in the Pathfinder Company he reported to the Hallmark Building in Pretoria where he was informed that he was now in the Corps of Signals, and so became the company's signals rep.

The colonel was so well established in this operational area that he had his own personal radio appointment title: 'Carpenter'. That name when transmitted over the airwaves made people sit up and listen. These regular two-hourly radio schedules only took a few minutes but it gave the crews a moment to brew tea. Continuing without further incident they arrived at the dropping-off point where Captain Ratte and his men set off on their mission.

Captain Velthuizen had an independent task to reconnoitre a particular road. It was necessary when carrying out a recce patrol to avoid contact with the enemy, so stealth and secrecy were the important principles. Watch the enemy, gain intelligence, and then get away undetected. After monitoring the road overnight the

Company Sergeant-Major Dennis Croukamp, with his notable service in the RLI where he was awarded the Bronze Cross of Rhodesia, spent many years in combat with the Selous Scouts, carrying out small-team recce patrols in Mozambique.

Using a helicopter mount, Dave Barr fitted twin .50-calibre Brownings to the colonel's Sabre.

After repeated failed attempts to get the 20mm cannon firing correctly it was replaced by a .50-calibre Browning.

pathfinders turned back and headed south, first to Okolongo then back to Okotopi, arriving home in the evening, tired but satisfied.

Gordon Brindley had an unusual experience in camp. While standing by the vehicle park he was hit in the sternum by an Owambo arrow. Momentarily stunned he watched it slowly droop and fall out; then looking up he saw Steve Bertrand on the other side of the Sabres holding a bow doubled over laughing. Needing to see how it worked he thought Gordon made an obvious target, but the subsequent altercation could have proved altogether more deadly had not Captain Peak arrived to keep them apart. On cooling down they all laughed at the ridiculousness of the moment.

The next day was Good Friday, 17 April, and the company was told by Colonel Breytenbach that they were going back into Angola. This first action was to be a dawn attack on a known SWAPO base. Following a preliminary SAAF air strike, the bush camp was to be assaulted by 32 Battalion with the pathfinders providing close support with their machine guns. Final preparations were made. There was no standard dress, and South African nutria-brown uniform mingled with Rhodesian camouflage and any other uniform available. Webbing was also left to individual preference. At last they set off, the colonel's command vehicle in the lead, heading north. After a few hours they crossed the cut line, and they were in Angola and feeling confident. There were no nerves and no apprehension about what lay ahead; only excitement at going into action with, what they thought, all the ace cards.

Navigation was extremely difficult because the land throughout this region was entirely flat, so the map showed no contour lines, no rivers nor any other aspect by which to take bearings. Only occasionally a dam would feature. These were built by the Portuguese to trap surface water and consisted of a big square hole in the ground with banked-up walls created with the dirt removed by the bulldozers. Later they would feature more prominently in the lives of the pathfinders.

Vast areas of wide-open savannah presented themselves to the lead vehicles but intruding into them were areas of thick, almost impenetrable bush. A tangled mass of dense thorn bushes stopped all forward progress, and aerial photographs were used to seek a route around the scrub. Keeping as much as possible in the open it did, however, become necessary on occasion to penetrate this natural obstacle and then a Unimog would be called to the front and that marvellous workhorse would crash in, bending and battering a road through for the others to follow.

Arriving at the rendezvous point radio communication was made with the 32 Battalion company providing the attack

Top left: The pathfinders were deployed in South West Africa to patrol the area of the Etosha Pan in Buffels. It proved to be a frustrating period with little result to show for their efforts.

Left: Lieutenant Verduin's Buffel. These troop-carrying vehicles were designed to withstand landmine blasts.

Above: The same Buffel after it had hit a Soviet mine laid by SWAPO; the vehicle crew and passengers escaped unharmed.

Top left and right: The pathfinders welcomed the move to the SAAF airfield at Ondangwa, but conditions were still basic and often the water was off. They were separated from 1 Parabat and everyone else on the base for that matter.

Centre: The Pathfinder Company struggled to maintain sufficient numbers to man the Sabre convoy, so 'stray' South Africans volunteered for pathfinder operations. Drinking proved a popular pastime with the men.

Left: Not allowed to mix with other units on the airfield, the company would braai their own meat each evening.

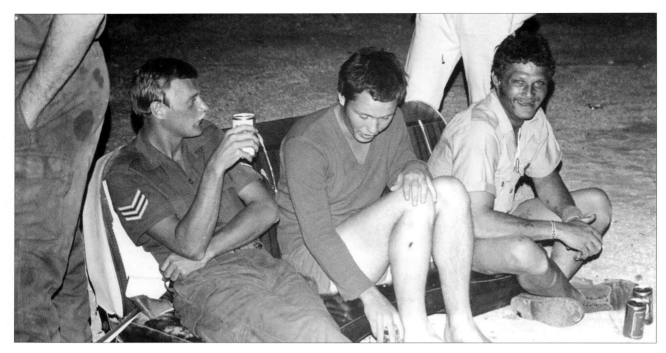

Sharing a good war story are Englishman Sergeant Gilly Gillmore, Canadian Sean Wyatt and Rhodesian John Wessels. In 1982 after the Pathfinder Company was disbanded, John Wessels and Sergeant Bob Beech were killed in a contact with Zimbabwean troops north of the Limpopo River. The circumstances of their mission, and deaths, are still a mystery.

troops. There was some apparent discrepancy about who was in the right location and who wasn't, so it was finally settled by firing flares into the sky, and at last light the two units linked up. But while it was a speedy solution to the problem it did not seem the wisest thing to do so close to the enemy. When not on guard duty the night was spent in disturbed sleep, the men confident but excited about the events to come.

Before dawn the next day, the terrorist camp began to buzz with activity. The enemy had discovered that something was up and soon speculative fire was being laid on likely approach routes with BM-21 multiple-barrel 122mm rocket launchers, but fortunately not where the South Africans actually were. However, the men felt the ground shake from the explosions of these large missiles. The air strike went in on schedule, and met anti-aircraft fire from several points around the camp.

The pathfinders put on their Kevlar helmets and the ground forces commenced their advance into the camp area. 32 Battalion formed a well-disciplined sweep line with the pathfinder vehicles spaced at intervals along it. If ever there was a test of courage it was to stand up and walk toward an unseen enemy position expecting any second to be shot at. The troops moved forward firing into likely enemy cover, but there was no return fire, and it soon became apparent that, apart from the anti-aircraft gunners, everyone else had fled.

While 32 Battalion dealt with two unexploded bombs that had been dropped by the Mirages on the initial strike, the Pathfinder Company moved out to clear the anti-aircraft gun positions. Supporting helicopters had reported seeing terrorists wheeling off heavy AA machine guns, but they located one gun position with three 14.5mm machine guns still intact. As the pathfinders drove to the site a SWAPO cadre, wounded in one leg and unable to escape, chose to shoot himself in the head. After checking for booby traps, the guns were lifted out by Puma helicopter.

Because the element of surprise had been lost, the attack was only a minor success, but the men were satisfied that they had done well on this, the first unit operation. In a very short while the Pathfinder Company reorganized and with

74

calmed nerves set off on the journey south, back to the border.

After the excitement of the operation and the expectation of more to come, things got a bit more stressful in the camp at Okotopi. The men soon received a warning order for another operation, so they made their preparations and moved by road to Ondangwa for the briefing, which was no sooner over than they were told it was cancelled. The same maddening situation repeated itself a couple of days later.

Frustration and boredom were causing complaint, and while the senior ranks maintained their silence the more junior members freely vented their spleens in the small PF bar of an evening, much to the annoyance of the host personnel. The pathfinders, whose combined military experience totalled hundreds of years in regular, reserve and conscripted armies, where not overly impressed with how they saw the National Servicemen being used and abused by the PF staff. To be always running about, stamping their feet in and standing to attention was absolutely correct for recruits but these were trained men on active service. It seemed outdated that the emphasis was all on obedience and that the true meaning of discipline had been overlooked, but that was apparently how the system worked. As a result the *uitlanders* were ever ready after a drink or two to side with the NS soldiers by deriding this aspect of the system.

The company foot-patrolling in Angola find convenient signs to prove it. This type of work was tough and demanding. The locals lived a primitive lifestyle and were harshly treated by whichever side thought they were giving comfort to the enemy. The soldier from the Owambo battalion (top right), an ex-SWAPO fighter, acted as interpreter.

Outrageous as their behaviour might appear it was no worse than that expected in any professional army, but it was just out of place in the austere SADF. A visiting colonel addressed the men, telling them that it didn't matter if they were killed as they were foreigners and therefore expendable. Such an attitude openly expressed by senior ranks was bound to have an effect on the attitude of the men.

That the Pathfinder Company had outstayed its welcome was becoming obvious to all, but that is not to say that the *uitlanders* weren't without their supporters. When work was needed to be done on the vehicles or weapons, assistance was asked for at army workshops or SAAF base workshops, the most complete cooperation that could ever be hoped for was given with tiffies being taken off other jobs to lend a hand.

Sergeant Gillmore would drive to Sector 10 headquarters to exchange u/s radio equipment and the conversation would go something like:

> Storeman: Saw your vehicles on the road the other day. Up to get SWAPO, were you?
> Gilly: No, things are a bit quiet at the moment.
> Storeman: Did you get many?
> Gilly: No, things are a bit quiet at the moment.
> Storeman: Okay, you can't talk about it. I quite understand.

Without doubt, individuals were taking satisfaction that, real or imagined, someone was aggressively taking the fight to SWAPO and not just reacting to their acts of terrorism. The pathfinders were lifting spirits all round just by being there.

Captain Velthizen gave a briefing and the next deployment would have the company patrolling in Buffels in the Etosha area to the west of Ondangwa. The change to Buffels, which were mine-proofed troop carriers, made sense but without a direct known threat why were they sent on such a routine low-risk task? The speculation was that they were simply being kept out of the way.

Dave Barr remembered: "We eventually found ourselves in the Etosha Pan and bounced around in the vehicles for ten hours a day in the heat. We were eating dust and becoming madder and meaner all the time."

One pathfinder had printed ace of spades cards but the men were threatened with severe punishment if they were ever dished out, so they never were, but remained a souvenir of those times.

Holding the FN MAG is American Rich Malson who joined the company without taking the selection process. He had enlisted independently in the SADF and not as part of any Rhodesian deal. Intending to sign up in 1 Recce Commando he was informed of this strange unit of foreigners, so arrangements were made for him to proceed to Okotopi where the original pathfinders were based. On hearing of his US military background the colonel accepted him into the company.

Day followed day without incident, the patrols stopping at villages and at the local *cuca* shops to check for any suspicious characters. It became known that this was all part of a plan by Sergeant Theunis Kruger who reappeared with his tame terrs after a long absence. One of the pathfinders, Rich Malson, clearly expressed his displeasure, as he later pointed out that "we would just as likely have found SWAPO activity in the Sea of Tranquillity as the Etosha Pan. It was rare to come across any human life (or animal for that matter) let alone insurgents". Rich was an ex-US Ranger who had some idea of what was productive soldiering and what was just buggering about. After that debacle Sergeant Kruger concentrated his efforts away from the men, but to be fair to him he was trying out an operating technique used successfully by the police Koevoet patrols, but how they fitted into this plan was never made absolutely clear to

Left: The new training schedule introduced by Major Alastair MacKenzie found the trainees on the border in the Caprivi Strip. Having passed the Drakensberg selection test the Pathfinder Company candidates were trained in SWAPO tactics, and here undergo interrogation at the end of the escape and evasion exercise.

A novel feature of the training camp was Terry, a lion who thought he was human, to the discomfort of some candidates to whom he took a liking. Orphaned as a cub Terry had been raised by men at a nearby Recce Commando camp. He would stroll out of the bush to take food from a nervous chef, and then collapse in a heap in the middle of a class receiving a lecture.

Locals found to have given succour to SWAPO would be punished by having their huts burned. The roofs burned fiercely when fully alight but fire was initially slow to take hold which gave the villagers time to remove their possessions.

the men whose sole motivation was their loyalty to the unit. Maintaining professional standards became harder as the days turned into weeks. Duties were carried out as required but their hearts were not in it, and various ribald songs and ditties expressed their appraisal of the situation and provided an outlet for their disappointment.

As the company stayed overnight at various camps they could see how much better conditions were for the CF companies on call-up, and the pathfinders found it easier to fit in and be accepted due to their similar ages and experiences, than in the camps with NS companies.

At one camp the men witnessed a quite unique event. An area near the perimeter wall was indicated for them to use and they bedded down on the ground for the night. By chance a company of 32 Battalion were also sleeping over, and on parade next morning one of their soldiers received punishment for serious misconduct involving a local woman. He was tied over an oil drum and whipped with a sjambok. It was exactly one hundred years since the British Army stopped flogging, but then Africa was always considered to be somewhat behind the rest of the world.

Colonel Breytenbach was not around at this time; his duties at 44 Parachute Brigade and his various other military involvements keeping him committed elsewhere. On their return to Okotopi it was the men's sense of humour, loudly expressed, which kept them going. But hope returned when there was announced a move to Ondangwa. This was welcomed because the SAAF airfield there was the centre of airborne operations and where a company of 1 Parabat was permanently on standby to be called out to any sighting of SWAPO.

The pathfinders did not expect to be spoilt by their new surroundings and they were not disappointed. The tents they were allocated were as far away from 1 Parabat and everyone else as was possible However, they were included in the midday meal arrangements in the mess hall but were given raw food to prepare their own main meal of the evening. The lunchtime meal was inevitably a variation of *mielie pap*, the staple diet that was tasteless and boring, so the men did what soldiers do and made a song up about it, which they sang in the mess hall, much to the amusement of the National Servicemen and the annoyance of the PF staff. On some occasions the kitchen actually ran out of food before everyone was fed.

The tents were comfortable enough; the top half of the tent walls could be dropped during the daytime heat, and raised again at night, though the temperature did not fall as much as it did in South Africa. There were no beds however and the men slept on the ground.

A new sergeant arrived in the company: Kevin O'Connor, ex-Irish Guards. Where he came from no one seemed to know, but he took on the camp admin and with the contacts he had already established was able to bargain and trade all sorts of extras for the company.

A warning order to be prepared to deploy was received but any cheering was soon quashed when it transpired that it was more Buffel patrolling. So the company returned to the previous area of operations and repeated the procedure of visiting the scattered *cuca* shops and villages to see if there was any likely terrorist presence. On one occasion two young men they checked out had every appearance of being SWAPO so they were taken to the police at Oshakati. But long hot, dry, dusty, boring days followed until a radio message flashed between call signs that one had hit a landmine.

This Buffel under the command of Lieutenant Verduin was one of 349 indiscriminate landmine incidents which occurred in 1981. This number decreased every year after that as a direct result of the South Africans' forceful actions into Angola. The Buffel performed exactly as it was designed to on hitting the mine: the explosion took off part of the chassis but the troop-carrying compartment fully protected its cargo. Shocked and shaken the men were without injury. Soon afterward the company was told that these internal patrols were at an end and they would not be required to perform them again, that they would be returning to Angola.

Back at Murrayhill things were progressing apace, and WOII McAleese had formed a new training team to instruct the CF paras on call-up. When an exercise or operation was planned using CF paratroopers, they assembled at Murrayhill to be intensively trained by WOII McAleese's team, who then deployed with them into combat. Great results were achieved and the team continued in existence long after the Pathfinder Company was disbanded.

The new batch of Pathfinder Company candidates trained under a new regime introduced by Major MacKenzie. The first part was still held in the Drakensberg Mountains, with the second tactical phase held at the Caprivi Strip near Mpacha. This region is the easternmost point of the South West African–Angolan border where it converges with Botswana and Zimbabwe. Here in the bush the trainees underwent in-depth familiarization of the enemy's culture, training and combat tactics. Finally, in an escape-and-evasion exercise their resistance to interrogation was tested. By being subjected to physical and mental stress, deprived of food, water and sleep, flaws in individuals would show that had so far been concealed. Only the best would be joining their colleagues in the company.

Back into Angola

At Ondangwa airfield the pathfinders' spirit returned as they prepared for a six-day foot patrol into Angola with UNITA. One reason for patrolling was to deny the ground to the enemy, the principle being that if you did not dominate it your enemy would. This work demonstrated to the men the depth of hatred between the two warring sides: any village even thought to be harbouring or supporting FAPLA was harshly dealt with by UNITA, just as a village supporting Savimbi was treated as equally cruelly by FAPLA. Because of the nature of this work these foot patrols became known unofficially to the men as 'Zippo patrols'.

This was a dirty war and it was the job of the patrols to find and shut down any SWAPO infiltration routes. They formed a number of fighting patrols which spread out through the area of operations. They worked independently but could support each other if contact was made.

Not all the pathfinders deployed on these patrols. A certain amount of administration and planning was taking place at base where Major MacKenzie arrived to see for himself how the war was being fought. The men in Angola fell under the control of Rhodesian Sergeant Bob Beech, the well-known ex-Anti-Tank Troop sergeant of the RLI, and the eldest of three brothers (unsurprisingly known as the Beech Boys) who had served in Support Commando.

The need for good personal organization was of paramount importance; and apart from ammunition everything they required was carried in their framed rucksack, the weight of which, often up to 40kg, being reminiscent of their Drakensberg selection days. Any item taken out for use was immediately returned when finished with because if they

Pro Patria Medal (1974)—for operational service (minimum 55 days) in defence of South Africa or in the prevention or suppression of terrorism ● issued for the Border War (counter-insurgency operations in South West Africa 1966–89) and for campaigns in Angola (1975–76 and 1987–88) ● the Cunene clasp was issued for the 1975–76 Angola campaign ● ribbon colours: national flag.

Southern Africa Medal (1989–)—for operational service outside South Africa and South West Africa since 1976 ● issued for Border War external operations and for the 1987–88 Angola campaign ● made of nickel from a captured Soviet tank ● ribbon colours: Angolan flag.

Gordon Brindley with a few souvenirs; the spear and arrows still used by the local population give an indication of the level of their subsistence. Gordon always had a camera to hand when others were reaching for their rifles, so many of the photographs used in this book are the result of Gordon's desire to record history as it happened.

Above and right: A wide variety of uniforms was worn when the company deployed on its own into Angola, with Rhodesian or communist camouflage preferred over the SADF nutria-brown issue kit. Webbing too was a matter of personal preference. No spare clothing was carried by the men, only sufficient to keep warm in the cold overnight temperatures.

Entering a kraal. The huts were searched for any signs of SWAPO, who would hide their weapons and uniforms and mingle with the villagers. If anything was discovered the the huts would be set alight. The local population suffered the interference of South African forces as they had previously suffered the intrusion of FAPLA, UNITA and Cuban forces.

had to move urgently there'd be no time to pack. A sleeping bag was a must during these winter months. While the daytime temperature was still blisteringly hot, at night it would drop drastically low.

Spare clothing was not taken, just sufficient to keep warm; there would be no washing or shaving until they returned. Rations, of course, were carried but the most important need was water. As well as their personal R4 rifles, M79 (bloopers) grenade launchers were carried by one man in four; it was designed to fire a variety of 40mm ammunition but only HE grenade rounds were taken and carried in a bandolier.

RPG-7 rocket launchers were also carried, as well as general-purpose machine guns, each man being required to carry extra ammunition belts. As it happened they did occasionally run out of food and Lang Price was once obliged to catch a pig and with deft use of a mortar tube kill it for roasting on the fire. Luckily, but unluckily for him, there was only one vegetarian in the company because the only food on the menu that night was bacon and crackling.

The pathfinders loaded a high proportion of tracer rounds in their rifle magazines because of the type of enemy contact they could expect to make. In conventional warfare contact would be initiated either by friendly forces or the enemy, where the firefight would be won or battle drills carried out until one side dominated. Because of the limited visibility in the African bush it often happened that the two sides would simply bump into each other. These simultaneous short-range encounters were sudden and ferocious with no time for fire-control orders or target-indication procedures, so those engaged relied on their tracer fire to signify the enemy position to their colleagues. The first few rounds in every magazine were tracer, and the magazine on the rifle might be fully loaded with tracer as a personal preference.

Long distances were expected to be covered on foot, and it was exhausting work carrying such heavy loads in the heat of the day, but the excitement of hitting the enemy at any moment was its own reward. As it happened no SWAPO were encountered during this time, and the only shooting taking place was back at Ondangwa.

One evening at Ondangwa airfield CSM Croukamp had found it necessary to discipline Sergeant O'Connor for the failure to bring back the stores he had been sent to collect. A heated argument led to the sergeant spitting at the CSM who responded by felling him with a head butt to the nose. O'Connor went away aggrieved and later returned in a highly agitated state but, not finding the CSM in his tent, took up his loaded rifle and went hunting for him. He found the CSM in the command post with Major MacKenzie, and sneaking behind the operators in the radio room he let rip a wild burst of shots into the corrugated-iron roof of the operations room.

With his rifle trained on his target, O'Connor demanded to see the commander of Sector 10, all the while focusing his hatred on the CSM. Major MacKenzie had to put all his hostage-negotiation skills learned in the SAS into practice. The brigadier in

The result of finding SWAPO. Bodies were searched for any information that might be carried, but first and with great care they were checked for booby traps. It was common practice in this type of fighting that any abandoned equipment or dead bodies would have a grenade with the pin removed placed underneath. This simple trap did cause fatal casualties to South African troops.

command of Sector 10 was sent for, and while they waited for his arrival the major heard out O'Connor's rants in an attempt to calm the situation.

Outside the post Mike Landskov with his FN and another pathfinder with his R4 covered the doorway. Mike had O'Connor covered the whole time through a crack in the wall but the hope was still to end the standoff without people being killed. Two hours passed and O'Connor remained as agitated as ever occasionally firing off automatic bursts from his 50-round magazine. Tensions rose to breaking point as the spluttering generator caused the lights to dim; the crazed Irishman thought it was part of a rescue plan and threatened to kill Croukamp then and there, but Major MacKenzie continued to gain O'Connor's confidence and persuaded him that the brigadier would not come while he was brandishing his rifle about, so he told him to keep his 9mm pistol but hand over his R4. As he did so a glimmer of a possibility presented itself and the officer lunged at the sergeant; the two wrestled over benches and onto the ground in a desperate struggle before the major eventually got the upper hand and disarmed O'Connor. CSM Croukamp's first reaction was to make a dash for the door but having reached it, on second thoughts, turned around to administer a few swift kicks to O'Connor's body. The action now over, the Irishman was arrested and taken away. He was later returned to South Africa where he, perhaps wisely, deserted.

Such was the reputation of the Pathfinder Company that the SAAF Orderly Officer who was unaware of the hostage situation sent a message to Colonel Breytenbach requesting him to instruct his men to stop firing through the hangar behind the command post because his tiffies were preparing aircraft for operations. The colonel said later that the request to stop shooting through the hangar sounded as if it was a regular para thing to do.

Returning from a tough foot patrol, and conscious of their low standing among the South African hierarchy this was the very last thing the company needed. The fact that Sergeant O'Connor came from elsewhere with few credentials and despite the determined efforts of the real pathfinders their standing must have been at absolute rock bottom. This incident came at a time when all foreigners in the SADF had come under the spotlight after the earlier actions of the

In camp at Ondangwa and on patrol in Angola the star vehicle of the Sabre convoy was Colonel Breytenbach's Toyota Land Cruiser with its twin .50-calibre Browning machine guns. Dave Barr had fitted the mounts and tuned the guns to a perfect pitch. As well as being the command vehicle it led the convoy on all patrols up to the time it was destroyed.

traitor Trevor Edwards. Edwards was known to many of the men. He had given up his fish and chip shop in Brighton on the south coast of England to sign up for the RLI, where after going through Training Troop he joined Support Commando toward the end of the war during the ceasefire period. He was one of a group of foreigners from the commando who did not wait for the official release date from the army but went absent early, and on joining the SADF were posted to 32 Battalion. After taking part in operations with the battalion he deserted and returned to Britain. His actions thus far did not make him a traitor but he then chose to go to the left-wing press with stories of atrocities allegedly carried out by the South Africans, which of course was music to the ears of their political enemies. After his accusations were splashed around the world he was invited to address a United Nations conference on matters on the troubled sub-continent. Why he chose to do this could have only been for one of two reasons: either he was honestly troubled by the reality of combat and the violence that is complicit with it or, like other soldiers before him, he chose to justify his cowardice by taking the moral high ground and denouncing his one-time colleagues as butchers and murderers. Either way, the actions of a traitor are neither forgotten nor forgiven, and even today no pathfinder would be saddened if his bloody corpse turned up in a darkened alley somewhere.

Back at camp the company was soon cleaned up and ready to deploy again. The colonel was back and advised that their next operation was to destroy a road. It was now widely recognized that FAPLA was so closely allied to SWAPO that

Pathfinder Company 44 Parachute Brigate: *The Philistines*

they too were a legitimate target, thus the task was to cut the tarred road that linked the large towns of Ongiva and Xangongo where FAPLA had an armoured brigade in residence.

Successful SAAF attacks on road traffic had forced the Angolan army to move its convoys at night; Colonel Breytenbach's plan was to mount a night ambush and to blow up two large culverts that ran under the road about five miles apart. The company would form two patrols: one patrol commanded by Major MacKenzie consisted of two Sabres and two Unimogs. Additionally, a new vehicle had joined the convoy, a one-and-a-half-ton Unimog (affectionately known as the Babymog) mounting one of the 14.5 heavy machine guns captured in the first vehicle deployment. The demolition of the easternmost culvert was the responsibility of Mike Landskov who was American Special Forces explosives-trained.

The other vehicles under command of the colonel would carry out the destruction of the western culvert. For the demolition job they had attached to them Sergeant van der Merwe, a large, brash South African engineer whose demeanour was that of a rear echelon base wallah, but first impressions could be deceiving.

The patrols practised their movement drills, taking up their ambush positions, and then the placing of the explosives. The South Africans had produced an epoxy substance with which to attach the explosives to the roof of the culvert but in the rehearsals it proved unsuccessful, so metal supports were fashioned to do the job. Mines would also be laid on the side of the road to damage any vehicle trying to bypass the spot. This was a war-ravaged part of a very poor country so no civilian transport was expected to be using the road. After three days of daytime and nighttime preparations they were ready to go.

The convoy set off heading north guided by the colonel in the lead Sabre; they crossed the cut line and arrived at a small UNITA camp, where they picked up guides who took them to a larger base about 30 kilometres into Angola. The officers checked maps and air photographs for the last time before the two groups split up on their separate missions. The bulk of the 120-kilometre journey would be carried out in daylight hours, arriving at the target area of the road after dark. The explosives would be put in place and the road ambushed until 0500 hours when, if no convoy was encountered the culverts would be blown and the patrols would then return to base.

Colonel Breytenbach's patrol was making good time when, on emerging from some bush into open savannah, they encountered three SWAPO guerrillas eating watermelons. The nearest Sabre opened up on them and in a moment it was all over. Their bodies lay scattered a few yards between them, the one corpse smoking and fizzling from the burning RPG-7 booster charges he was carrying, ignited by the chest-load of R4 tracer rounds put there by the young Rhodesian 'Irish' Mahon. No other enemy was spotted: these three appeared to be a stray group, but the patrol was cheered by this small victory early into the operation; apart from Sergeant van der Merwe who suddenly remembered he had a foot injury and asked if he could go back to camp. The colonel explained to him in simple terms that this was a group of foreigners who went into action with no backup and no casevac facilities, so injured or not he stayed.

The patrol continued north and slightly east, to continue on this heading until it came to the road. Darkness fell and the stars came out; most prominent among the constellations was the Southern Cross by which the pathfinders knew to be guided if they found themselves separated and needing to head south. In single file the patrol vehicles progressed through open savannah, the drivers not needing their night-vision goggles owing to a full moon. Suddenly ahead of them, only a few hundred yards away, appeared a line of lorries moving from right to left: the road.

Moving more cautiously now the Sabres manoeuvred into position to ambush the road, and a foot patrol set off to locate the culvert. It was quickly found but instead of preparing it as planned Sergeant van der Merwe dug a hole into the embankment on the side of the road. The men then packed about 425lbs of explosives and all the mines into the hole, set the charges, and returned to the ambush position to wait for a convoy to arrive.

Major MacKenzie's patrol similarly made good progress on their way to their target, which was made slightly more

Top A daylight rehearsal for Major MacKenzie's patrol to destroy the road between Ongiva and Xangongo; further rehearsals took place after dark in order that the demolition party and the ambush party were thoroughly versed in their roles.

Above: An addition to the convoy was this one-and-a-half-ton Unimog carrying one of the three Soviet 14.5mm machine guns captured in the pathfinders' first camp attack. Known as the 'Babymog' it rolled quite dramatically when the gun was fired.

Above: New Zealander, ex-SAS Major Alastair MacKenzie joined 44 Parachute Brigade as 2IC Operations and Training. He demanded only the highest standard of soldiering from the men.

difficult due to the need of avoiding kraals en route. The patrol included a small contingent of UNITA fighters travelling in one of the Unimogs, who guided the patrol safely through the area until about 2200 hours when the Unimog driven by Ken Gaudet had its petrol tank yanked off by a tree stump. The patrol laagered in an all-round defence while they tried to repair the damage. Suddenly single warning shots were fired nearby and returned from other positions: the local home guard had been alerted that something was amiss. These local militia would warn FAPLA and other villages in the district of any possible threat in their area.The major took a calculated risk and ordered the vehicle lights switched on and as much noise as possible made in the hope they would be taken for FAPLA. The UNITA fighters sang their *chimurenga* songs, which aided in the deception. The plan worked and they made good their vehicle repair and got on their way, with no further militia warning shots being heard.

Sergeant Dean Evans in full Rhodesian camouflage (top photo) with some UNITA fighters who, while not the best soldiers in Africa, proved invaluable to the pathfinders when a Unimog became incapacitated in enemy territory.

On locating the objective the patrol carried out their rehearsed procedures. Mike Landskov took his measured amount of explosives (plus a bit extra) and fitted them to the high roof of the culvert.

One enemy vehicle did drive along the colonel's stretch of road before the other ambush was fully in place so the ambush party took cover and allowed it through. A long cold night passed without further activity. At five o'clock the following morning the charges were blown. Mike Landskov's was a complete success, but Sergeant van der Merwe's only partially so. His hurried affair left most of the road untouched and still passable, but with all the explosives spent there was nothing else that could be done.

The major's team planted their landmines and the two patrols set off southward independently. After and hour or so Colonel Breytenbach called a halt and then doglegged back to lay in ambush on the tracks left by his vehicles. If FAPLA came in pursuit they would have a surprise waiting for them, but after a few hours it became clear there was no pursuit so the colonel continued south.

Major MacKenzie's patrol did have a distant sighting of FAPLA on their journey home, just as one of the Unimogs bizarrely disappeared into a hole in the ground. What the hole was for was unclear but the vehicle fitted it perfectly with almost no space around the sides. With the unmistakable rumble of armour to the north the major considered torching and abandoning the Unimog, and risk suffering the colonel's displeasure, coupled with dark mutterings about the *uitlanders* from the army staff at Oshakati. However, after numerous attempts the other Unimog trying to tow it out took off 'at the double' and the trapped vehicle shot out of the hole like a SAM-7 missile. A burst of 14.5 in FAPLA's direction dulled whatever enthusiasm FAPLA might have had for getting any closer.

Passing south through UNITA territory the pathfinders crossed the cut line into South West Africa and back to Ondangwa. The colonel held a debriefing where his disappointment at the lack of success was made clear; he was a man used to success. An added frustration was the number of times vehicles had got stuck, either in soft sand or muddy vleis, and had had to be repeatedly towed out. This was a result of the terrain and not a fault with the vehicles but it was nevertheless a cause for concern as a mission could be put in jeopardy because of this. Also, the puncture-proof filling in the tyres had proved ineffective against the savage thorns of the African bush which had caused interminable delays when tyres had to be changed.

Captain Sumner was a new arrival at the unit. An American he had served in tanks before joining the Rhodesian Armoured Car Regiment. His appearance at Ondangwa was welcomed because he was able to organize beds for the company, as well as improving the standard of food.

The .50-cal machine guns on the Land Cruisers produced a considerable concussion when fired, and because the barrel muzzle was only a couple of feet away from the heads of the driver and commander the colonel told Dave Barr to do something about it. Having already established a good working relationship with the air force personnel Dave asked if they could suggest anything. They had previously tried a twin gun-mounting in their Puma helicopters but it had proved too much for the airframe. So taking one of these mounts and modifying it in their workshops it was fitted onto the command Sabre; the gun shield

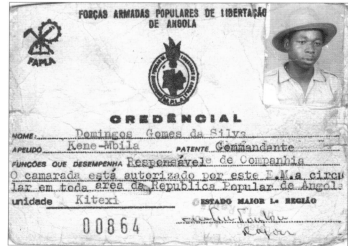

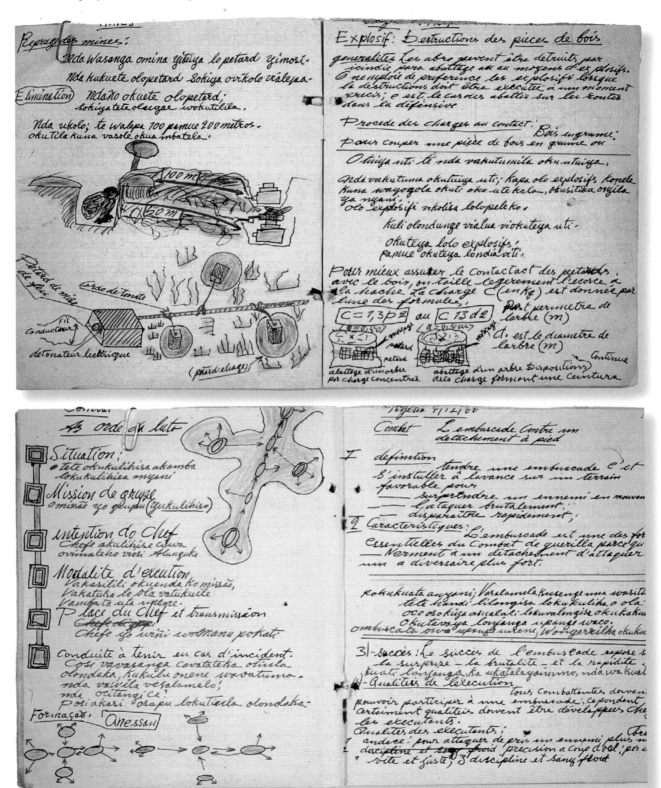

Enemy documentation gathered on patrol was passed back to Military Intelligence for collation.

had to be removed and a second .50-cal Browning was then mounted next to the first. An empty sandbag arrangement was then fitted to catch the empty cases, because an avalanche of red-hot *doppies* cascading into the back of the vehicle was not desirable. A communist sight recovered from a 14.5 anti-aircraft machine gun was fitted, and on test-firing proved to be an absolute joy of balance and controllability.

Dave was due to go back to Pretoria for a spell of R&R but not before he beat up a black Owambo soldier who had pushed in at the meal queue. For the middle two weeks of June nothing happened; the men really needed to be active on operations because being idle in camp was just a recipe for trouble. Their kit was prepared for combat, they were prepared for combat, but the days were spent lounging on their beds and drinking in the evening.

It was reported that a UNITA camp had been attacked and the Pathfinder Company was tasked to hunt for any FAPLA who might be still in the area. They received the warning order on 29 June. Major MacKenzie commanded the company who mounted up and headed north, once again crossing the cut line in the early hours of 1 July.

At the end of the first day inside Angola the company carried out its usual 'last light' procedure. This tactic involved stopping at one dummy location before moving into a different overnight position when the daylight had faded. The vehicles then laagered in all-round defence and the men remained stood-to until the order was passed along to stand down, when the nighttime routine commenced. While one man from each section remained on guard his colleagues could eat. There were no fires or lights, just something cold from a tin, and then into a sleeping bag next to the Sabres. Everyone remained fully dressed and their weapons to hand.

Sentries were relieved through the night until half an hour before dawn, when the camp was silently woken, and the men moved into their stand-to defensive positions, remaining there until half an hour after sunrise. Then, leaving a sentry on duty the sections would brew up and have breakfast. One section was sent on a clearance patrol, a 360-degree sweep of the surrounding area. The patrol had been gone a while when a distant flurry of shots alerted the camp that something was up. A tense few moments were spent waiting by the radio, before Jay's voice came on. It was nothing to worry about: the patrol had spotted a figure in camouflage trying to hide and had shot him. But it was just a *madala* (Shona term of respect for an old man) in a flowery shirt. The major asked how badly he was hit; there was a pause on the radio then Jay came back on and said he had died.

Civilian casualties are an unavoidable feature of warfare. In the Rhodesian bush war villagers learned to go out into an open field as soon as they became aware of military action in their area. As exposed as they were when the shooting started it was better than hiding and being shot as a terrorist.

The company continued on its mission to hunt for FAPLA but after fruitlessly following up various spoor in the camp location they concluded that no enemy remained in the area, and so returned south.

On 3 July a public holiday celebration was being held at Oshakati, with sports events, arena displays and family activities. Dave Barr was invited to take part in a freefall parachute demonstration, and when completed he had drinks bought for him and was made to feel most welcome. He returned to Ondangwa and suggested that everyone should go and enjoy the festivities.

The men got cleaned up and properly dressed, then loaded onto a lorry for the short journey. Arriving at the celebrations, the pathfinders immediately got into the party spirit, but unfortunately only moments after their arrival one South African singled out Londoner Paul Whitehead for attention; this individual apparently had a fascination for tattoos of which Paul displayed many. Now, Paul was an ex-RLI man and though slow to rile he would react if pushed. It may have been that the South African was used to bullying National Servicemen and was fooled by Paul's average height and slim

94

build but soon the disparaging comments turned to prodding the swallows on Paul's neck. Paul was then obliged to dish out a sound thrashing which included the removal of part of the bully's ear. The Philistines were told to leave.

The day was not a total disaster; on their return to Ondangwa the CSM of the Parabat company had a braai waiting as a special tribute to the pathfinders, the next day being Independence Day for the Americans. A kind gesture that was appreciated by the men who responded by being, more or less, well behaved for the remainder of the day.

First casualties

The next morning, while nursing some severe hangovers, the unit received the order to prepare again for deployment. The mission was to dominate an area of Angola by multiple foot patrols in conjunction with a Parabat company. They were soon packed and ready to go. Attached to them was a soldier from the local Owambo battalion who would act as interpreter. This deployment was the result of a suggestion by CSM Croukamp:

> I was on the carpet in front of Brigadier Badenhorst, being taken to task for the lack of discipline in the Pathfinder ranks, which I personally thought was merely high spirits. I suggested that he gave us a chunk of real estate in Angola and leave us there indefinitely; that way we would not upset him and his HQ staff. I also suggested that on resupply day, normally every ten days, he allowed five troops back out on R&R, giving them those ten days off; but the deal would be that he sent them back to Pretoria and not leave them in base in the operational area to compound his problem. The Cunene River would be our western boundary with our patrol area stretching some thirty kilometres to the east; we were restricted to about twenty kilometres into Angola.

The South African engineer officer Lieutenant Brown had been supervising the selection training in the Caprivi Strip. He arrived at Ondangwa and was given command of one of the eight-man patrols; his second-in-command was Dave Barr who recorded the start of the mission:

> We got onto Buffels, travelled up to the cut line and then went west for about 15 kilometres, to find a particular

Top: Peter Morpuss, after passing selection, remained as a medic instructor for the following course. On joining the company he was flown straight into Angola on foot patrol.

Above: Ex-US Ranger Rich Malson.

Pathfinders enjoy a moment's rest in the shade, out of the blistering sun.

Ex-US Airborne Ken Gaudet.

beacon that we would use to enter Angola. That was where our navigation would start; we got lost and finally found it at about 1030 hours that evening. We dismounted the Buffels and moved into Angola on foot, to start what was to be a three-week-plus operation. Major MacKenzie led us unerringly until about 0430 hours the next morning, when we stopped and he told me to proceed in a certain direction for 200 metres and see if I could find a particular dam. I did as he said and sure enough there it was. He had navigated us 25 miles at night with no landmarks right to our destination, which was a dam, about 50 metres square. This is where we stopped and rested for a couple of hours. We had been up since 0615 hours the previous morning, right up till dawn the following morning. Our backs ached and our feet were sore.

Lieutenant Brown's first task was to put in place an overnight ambush on another dam, and as his patrol proceeded to the location they came across a young Owambo who the guide said was SWAPO. Taking him prisoner, he was used to lead the patrol to the dam. At first he took them off course but after being given firm advice about his future conduct and what the penalty might be, he fully co-operated.

Locating the dam, the patrol based up as a recce team went forward to plan the ambush position. Four men with the guide and prisoner remained in the base overnight while the other four team members set the ambush. At 2100 hours four enemy guerrillas approached the dam and the ambush party opened up, killing one, while the others escaped.

The pathfinders linked up with Golf Company, 32 Battalion.

Next morning, after the routine stand-to in the base camp, the ambush site was checked and the identity of the casualty was confirmed as SWAPO. Returning to base camp Dave Barr took an entrenching tool and moved into the bush to perform his ablutions when he saw a wide-eyed black face looking at him from the bush to his front. Pandemonium ensued as firing immediately commenced, with the spade being shot out of Barr's hand. As well as small-arms fire the pathfinders were being hit with mortars and RPG rockets. They had to get out quickly and with Lieutenant Brown leading they withdrew to new positions, but not before the prisoner was hit and killed, and young Sean Wyatt wounded in the leg. The officer's radio was also shot up and had to be abandoned.

Having moved back some distance they then stopped and turned around to cover some open ground which would have given them a clear shot at any pursuers, However, the lieutenant again withdrew, and they kept going until two patrols led by Major MacKenzie and CSM Croukamp linked up to reinforce them. Gordon Brindley was nearby when the contact started and has a clear recollection of that moment:

> I was with Lieutenant Fred Verduin some kilometres away on a parallel patrol with two other lads when we heard the tremendous sound of what seemed like crackling twigs in a hot fire. After a few loud thumps we realised that there was a hondo [battle] going on, so we raced off in the direction of the firing with full kit and packs. Fred galloped along with his long legs pumping like a racing camel, with the other three members of the patrol desperately trying to keep up with him. We eventually got to the scene of the ambush as I met Sean who was very proud of a shrapnel cut on his thigh, telling me how an enemy rifle grenade had landed full square in the middle of his back, and had exploded after rolling down next to his leg! He was extremely lucky.

With the major now in command the reunited company swept over the vicinity of the earlier contact and the dam. A helicopter had been requested and after flying over the area was able to confirm that there were no SWAPO to be seen. There was, however, an old base camp sited close to the dam, and it was from there that the enemy had been able to mount such a fast and aggressive response. Much later, information from intercepted SWAPO radio transmissions filtered down to the company that as many as 36 enemy had been hit during the contact.

Next morning a helicopter was called in to casevac Sean Wyatt. The major also left on it, as did Lieutenant Brown who was not seen in the company again. CSM Croukamp was then given command of the mission. The men had been disappointed with the lack of aggression shown by their officer during the contact; however, they were now under the CSM, and with his years of experience in the Selous Scouts carrying out just this sort of external operation, they had every hope of a rematch with a more satisfactory result. Englishman Peter Morpuss had arrived at Ondangwa in time to meet the helicopter bringing back the wounded Sean Wyatt. Pete had passed an earlier selection course but as a medic he had stayed behind with the next course as the instructor. He had moved to Rhodesia in April 1977 to join the Grey's Scouts, but after a year got a transfer to the Rhodesian Light Infantry and joined Support Commando, Anti-Tank Troop. He was parachute-trained in August 1978, and passed the Troop Medics course. He completed his service in the RLI in April 1980 and went to live in Cape Town before someone from 44 Parachute Brigade contacted him with news of his former RLI comrades. So he signed up. Peter's disgust at the poor living standards at Ondangwa was only short-lived as he was immediately flown out to join the company in Angola where, as well as his medic pack, he was given an RPG-7 rocket launcher to carry.

Patrolling continued, with the eight-man sticks operating independently and spread thinly over a large area. Each patrol would have to handle alone whatever enemy came their way. Motivation and morale were good as they searched for any sign of SWAPO activity; kraals were visited and searched, with eight to ten miles being covered each day. No enemy was

Only the Cunene River provided fresh running water; all other rivers were dry, with the only other local source of water being polluted dams.

encountered but the pathfinders pressed on, keen to make contact and spurred on by the excitement of flushing out the enemy deep in his own country.

Prior to each resupply CSM Croukamp requested permission to extend their area of operations, and was subsequently permitted to move another ten kilometres north but no farther.

As the days turned into weeks the discomfort of this work, what with the hundred-pound loads the pathfinders were carrying, made itself more apparent. Some men wore Rhodesian Army clandestine takkies. These were high-leg canvas boots with smooth rubber soles designed not to leave tracks, and while comfortable they were not up to such constant hard work, being flimsy and of poor quality. Dave Barr's takkies had started to come apart and had to be taped up. Without a change of clothing the men's dishevelled appearance was matched by a tramp-like smell. Dave Barr remembered the part water played in this:

> For water we had to go to so-called little dams, which were basically mud holes where the animals drank water. The animals also urinated in the water at the same time. The water had the colour of muddy urine and tasted like urine. We would put water purification tablets in and I never had a problem with dysentery or anything like that. Our perspiration smelled like urine, our uniforms were like cardboard and smelled like urine and perspiration, but that was due to the water we had to drink: we had no choice, otherwise we would just dehydrate. It was hot so we would drink about six one-litre water bottles a day. At night it was freezing cold, but we went to the dams every day and usually sent out a watering party to fill the bottles.

Occasionally distant firing would be heard but always out of the pathfinders' area of operations, and over the radio they would hear reports of contacts made by the Parabat company, so frustrations were starting to creep in. Searching one kraal, ex-Parachute Regiment Mark Griffiths found an 1850s' Tower percussion musket, and recognizing the historic value of the piece decided to rescue it for posterity. Dave Barr also took a fancy to it and after persuading Mark that he really didn't want to be carrying the thing throughout the rest of the patrol bought it from him for R15.00. Dave kept the rifle which was hung over the mantelpiece at home in California.

Back in South West Africa the Pathfinder Company headquarter element was based at Ombalantu, one of those forward company bases. They received radio requests from the men for boots, trousers and other basic items. They were unable to fulfil these requests so the men just had to get on with what they had and sort things out for themselves.

One day a pathfinder patrol met up with another patrol from the Parabats and, forming a night-time patrol base, Alan Cauvin went out with a couple of others to seek fresh food. Until now their hot meals consisted of whatever was in their ration-pack tins all mixed together and curried, so a lot of curry powder was consumed. They came across an African goat herder and offered him some chocolate in exchange for one of his beasts. Not surprisingly the herder was reluctant until Alan, who was a big man, leered down at him and the man quickly realized the sense in accepting the offer. The goat was shot and a fire lit for the braai.

There were remnants of a past civilization as Dave Barr recalled:

> One afternoon Lang and I were sent up to an old abandoned town. The place had shown prosperity at one time, but now was nothing more than a rubbish heap with burned-out vehicles in the streets. We had to do an OP over the Cunene River. We moved through in the middle of the night and came across pockmarked walls and the signs of destroyed prosperity. We thought to ourselves, "Once upon a time

A pathfinder patrol linked up with one from 32 Battalion. This battalion, made up of ex-FNLA guerrillas, had been formed by Colonel Breytenbach at the end of the Angolan war following Portugal's withdrawal from the continent. Superior MPLA and Cuban forces had driven the pro-Western FNLA from the country. Colonel Breytenbach had previously served as an advisor to Holden Roberto's FNLA; WOII Peter McAleese had also worked with the organization but as a commander of the British mercenaries hired to bolster the FNLA. The existence of 32 Battalion was not widely known but to those serving on the border they were highly regarded as tough fighters who spearheaded many of the camp attacks. Here they have arrived at a vlei where rainwater has pooled and allowed them to collect what fresh water they can. They are armed with Soviet weapons and are dressed in their own distinctive camouflage uniforms, which reflect a Portuguese influence. Webbing equipment too was of their own design.

people danced and sang here, had family get-togethers and now it is all gone; only the ghosts of the past move around here." It was very eerie moving through these villages in the middle of the night—they were totally empty.

We would occasionally search a kraal, do an OP on it for about an hour or so and if we saw anything suspicious, we would go in and search the place. This was something I detested because they were filthy inside. Everything stank and every time we opened anything that had any clothes in it, cockroaches would come running out.

Old SWAPO base camps were happened upon occasionally and two suspected terrorists were captured but nothing substantially rewarding was returned for the effort being put in. Helicopters resupplied the company with rations, sometimes bringing replacement personnel; even a couple CF paras on call-up were added to the manpower. Rob Gilmour was returned to camp after developing a bad case of tick bite fever, taking with him Dave's musket for safekeeping. No helicopters were available at a time when the company needed redeploying to another area farther north, so the convoy of Sabres manned by a skeleton crew of pathfinders from Ombalantu drove up for the task, commanded by Captain Sumpter. Because they had to carry everything, the fresh water they were supplied with on this occasion was only sufficient for one day or so and then it was back to the cattle urine. Gordon Brindley later recalled how he managed:

I kept my intake down to around a litre and a half a day, despite carrying a heavy pack (around 40kg) in the heat of Angola. Water discipline was strictly enforced during Training Troop in the RLI and

Helicopter resupply kept the men in rations and water but only enough for a few days as everything had to be carried on long foot patrols; they were already weighed down with a large amount of weapons and ammunition.

this experience really helped when it came to operating in rigorous conditions of active service. We were taught to drink well at first light and abstain during the heat of the day since the water merely was wasted in the form of sweat. Water was drunk again at last light in order for the body to absorb it efficiently. Of course, if we came to a source of water during the day we drank as much as we could before moving off again.

One time, faced with the prospect drinking green slimy cow urine, he chose to recycle his own:

The best tip in drinking urine is never, NEVER try and make hot tea out of the stuff. It is disgusting! The best way is to leave it overnight until it gets fairly cold. Then mix in some of the Ready Maid powdered orange drink, which was in our rat packs. Drink immediately and the taste isn't too unpleasant.

Intelligence from radio transmissions was passed to the company, who learned that three SWAPO had been killed in a contact with the Parabat company; the next day another contact produced six kills for the Parabats. The pathfinders were more than envious of their South African colleagues. On top of it all 32 Battalion had carried out a successful camp attack, killing 75 terrorists.

CSM Croukamp and the men wanted to cross the Cunene River where gook-hunting would be productive but orders from Oshakati forbade such a move. It was believed that Headquarters did not want to provoke a confrontation with FAPLA, but after three weeks of stinking and with their clothes rotting off them the emaciated pathfinders were getting desperate to provoke a fight with someone. The CSM moved the company away from the flat land to the banks of the Cunene River, where some higher ground and the river itself presented a better defensible position. He made it known to the local population that they would be based in the area for some time. If he could not find SWAPO, maybe he could get them to come to him.

The company formed a patrol base with better trenches than the shell scrapes they would normally dig, and a tactical plan was worked out with Sergeant Bob Beech's section defending the area most likely to be used for the enemy's approach. Other sections rehearsed counter-attack drills to cover every eventuality. Higher vigilance was maintained with increased sentry activity. After stand-to on the second day the morning clearance patrol carried out its usual 360-degree sweep of the area but on this occasion found spoor of an enemy recce patrol. The CSM moved the company south about three kilometres to a new position and dug in once more. With the CSM having worked with Sergeant Beech during the earlier days of the Rhodesian bush war, Beech again was given the side most likely to come under attack. Peter Morpuss made an entry in his diary for 25/26 July:

> 25 July: We are staying in camp while Sergeant Beech's stick go out and patrol. So today should be a nice and relaxing day if nothing happens. Had some pickled fish last night, farting so bad it stank me out of my sleeping bag.

> 26 July: The gooks hit us about 5 o'clock this morning. They threw everything at us including 82mm and 60mm mortars and RPG-7s. Kept mortaring us for about 20 minutes. Fortunately most of the mortars were going over our positions. The RPGs were more of a problem because they were hitting the trees around us, showering us with shrapnel. The rounds were coming in low as well, at head height. I was cursing that I hadn't dug a proper trench.

SWAPO launched the well-planned attack during the last stag of the night sentry before everyone had been awakened for stand-to. Approximately 60 mortar bombs were fired in the general direction of the patrol base, and as the mortar barrage diminished ferocious small-arms and machine-gun fire were exchanged at short range. New Zealander Gary 'Kiwi' Watson also wished he had dug a deeper hole. Carrying the radio, he had only dug the shell scrape deep enough to get the set below ground. And now the CSM, as usual wanting to be in the thick of the fighting, arrived on top of him.

Sergeant Beech fired off the anti-personnel claymore mines which had an immediate effect and the intensity of the enemy's fire decreased. In the semi-darkness CSM Croukamp rallied his men. Lieutenant Verduin's eight-man stick then stood up and swept forward toward the enemy position only 20 metres or so ahead. After their bold advance the SWAPO fighters turned and withdrew, and the firing stopped.

CSM Croukamp remembers:

> Suddenly everything went quiet. So far the action had taken about half an hour. I had been hit by shrapnel from an earlier rifle grenade when it had hit a tree behind me. I could feel the wet from my blood in the small of my back; other than that it was numb. We lay there, hyped up after this intense contact, shouting abuse at the enemy. I called for quiet and asked for a casualty report, but before any of the section commanders could reply we heard the distinct doof of a mortar bomb going off, which signalled the start of yet another mortar bombardment. It had been about 20 minutes since the firing had stopped.

It was now that the pathfinders picked up most of their mortar shrapnel injuries. Peter Morpuss was the only man in the advancing sweep line not to be hit and being the medic he spent an hour patching up the others. Two men he could do little for were Rhodesian Carl Saltzman and American Rich Malson who each had shrapnel in an eye. They would require further treatment and both would permanently lose the sight of their respective damaged eyes.

Another man Pete could not aid was Englishman Steven Hadlow who lay dead in his trench. As SWAPO began their withdrawal, a grenade had gone off next to him, killing him instantly. Steve had not long passed the selection course where Pete had been an instructor; he had only joined the company in Angola days before. He left a widow, Debbie, back in Pretoria.

One of the wounded had a particular gripe. Kiwi Watson had actually completed his service contract five days previously but had been unable to get airlifted out. To add to insult to injury he later found out that he wasn't even getting paid for this extra time as his wages had been stopped on the exact date his contract was up.

Left: Immediately after the contact, the medic Peter Morpuss patches up Dave Barr. Eight wounded were casevaced to South West Africa but apart from Rich Malson and Carl Saltzman who suffered eye injuries they all returned to combat duty.

Facing left: Steve Hadlow shortly before being killed by a grenade in a contact with SWAPO.

Lieutenant Fred Verduin and Dave Barr safely back in South West Africa.

CSM Croukamp summed up the contact:

> On our side one dead and eight wounded. On the enemy side after first light we found one dead; depressing. Following up we found the mortar base-plate position, with a lot of blood in various positions and a number of bloody swabs and bandages lying around which made us all feel a bit better. Once back at our main base we learned through enemy radio intercepts that we had killed 12 and wounded 12. After that I felt much better about the contact. It had been one hell of a night. Within our camp one could not take a pace in any direction without one's foot being within an inch or two of a mortar tail fin; a mixture of Soviet 60mm and 82mm mortar tail fins, amounting to over 200 mortar bombs. From the signs left at the base-plate position it had taken them a long time to set up, possible starting at daylight the previous day.

Radio contact was lost during the contact because mortar explosions had cut the diapole antenna, but a quick repair was made and Oshakati was informed of the situation. Alouette helicopters soon arrived to casevac the worst of the wounded, and also to take Hadlow's body back to the military hospital at Oshakati. Two sections followed up the spoor left by the retreating SWAPO, but returned after reaching the northern extremity of their area. The reorganized company then moved south until they were instructed over the radio to prepare for uplift back to South West Africa. Captain Sumpter was to fly out in the first helicopter but while they were waiting for uplift he suggested in true South African fashion that they should have a braai. A nearby kraal was visited and ration tins were exchanged for a scrawny goat. As before, the goat owner was reluctant; he had apparently never seen tin cans before because he put one in his mouth in an attempt bite it. The meat was tough and full of gristle so perhaps he had the last laugh.

The men returned first to Ombalantu where they enjoyed their first good night's sleep in three weeks; then back to camp at Ondangwa where a rest, a proper braai, and plenty of cold beers were enjoyed.

It was announced on muster parade on the morning of 28 July that several of the men would be going back to Pretoria for various military courses. Throughout the day the men sorted out their admin issues: some went to Oshakati to draw pay, others raised the floor level of their tents having been told that the area where they were living flooded in the rainy season. Weapons and the specialist stores and equipment were cleaned and checked, ready for future use. Getting the laundry done was another high priority.

Captain Peak had earlier taken a stray pig under his protection, and which had become a popular feature of the Pathfinder Company's camp. Named FUP (Fat Useless Pig) by the men it was a source of amusement when all else failed. On the evening of the 29th a variety show was put on at the air base for the troops of Sector 10. The pathfinders arrived already well lubricated and ready for a good time. The show was not really up to international standards so, to liven things up, one Philistine released FUP onto the stage where it careered around knocking over speakers and creating general mayhem. The scattering performers were nonplussed, and much merriment ensued.

After a couple of false starts the men on course eventually got their flight back to South Africa, with the C-130, called a 'Flossie' by the South Africans, taking them to Waterkloof AFB near Pretoria where they were met by Captain Velthuizen who informed them of the specific courses they would be attending. Most were to go on a FAC (forward air controller) course at the Aviation Institute, while others went on a demolition course. It was a Saturday and they arrived at Murrayhill in time to hit the pub. The next morning they were off duty so by 8 o'clock some were at the beer again. Others went to 1 Military Hospital at Voortrekkerhoogte in Pretoria to check on Rich Malson and Carl Saltzman who had been admitted for treatment to their eye injuries.

Military hospitals were run quite differently from their civilian equivalents. Staff fitted into the army rank structure and discipline was still expected although generous leeway was allowed for badly hurt soldiers. Patients were expected to help out with various light duties if able. The treatment was thorough and comprehensive with no hurry to discharge men back to their units.

Visiting times were rigidly enforced and visitors were expected to behave in a sedate manner so as not to disturb the other patients. However, as the hospital became more accustomed to treating members of the Pathfinder Company, the ward staff tended to accommodate their visitors by shutting themselves in their offices until they had gone. By turning a blind eye to the more raucous behaviour and the amount of booze that was being brought in, a mutual respect developed between the staff and patients.

The men were surprised to discover that Major MacKenzie had left the army. Because his engagement was not part of the deal for the ex-Rhodesians he was not eligible for the same housing allowances, with the result that all his pay was going on paying his rent. So reluctantly he resigned and returned home.

Conditions at Murrayhill had not noticeably improved during the men's absence, but some individuals were making an attempt to lighten the atmosphere as ex-Scots Guardsman Colin Brown recalls:

> After the staff sergeant who was in charge of the cookhouse realized that he could get home at night instead of sleeping at the camp he left us to our own devices, and I believe we improved the lot of the lads and the food one hundred percent. It was always nice to have some of the pathfinders back from the bush and we would always go out of our way to give them what they wanted before they redeployed. Rhodesian 'Bonzo' as the name suggests was a bit of a lad, and as we settled into the routine even the colonel was impressed with the standard of food and the general running of the kitchen. It was

customary to break at 10 o'clock, and in the South African army this constituted a cup of chicory coffee and Ouma rusks, which were as tough as a 'hardtack' biscuits and had to be dunked into the coffee to soften up, otherwise you would break your teeth on them.

After a hard day slaving over a hot stove, Bonzo and I hatched a plot to liven up the coffee break. We would make some 'cookies' for the morning break using local *dagga* (marijuana) and chocolate-drink powder as flavouring. After a few failed attempts they came out looking like chocolate chip cookies and we were impressed with the results. Next day we laid out the table that the colonel and Sergeant-Major Muller usually sat at and Bonzo approached with two cups of coffee which he placed down in front of them both, explaining that due to rats in the store (we lost so much food to them) there were no rusks but we had baked them some biscuits instead. They were both deep in conversation and after taking

Captain Graham Peak with his pet pig FUP. It was eventually killed and eaten; the pathfinders were not overly big on sentimentality. Captain Peak started his military career in 1974 as a National Serviceman in the Rhodesian SAS. On completion, he started regular service, taking an officer's course at the School of Infantry, Gwelo. He then served in the Rhodesian Army Service Corps. After the fall of Rhodesia he applied for an operational post in the SADF and was sent to 44 Parachute Brigade.

their first mouthful looked across and nodded their appreciation. As time went on the conversation got louder and louder and after about 30 minutes they both started laughing, which got louder and louder as they called for more coffee. Both of them were sliding off the benches as the conversation got funnier and funnier. After an hour they both decided it was time to go back to work and stood up, almost falling over the benches laughing. The colonel headed over to Bonzo and me and held out his hand and thanked us for taking the time to make him biscuits for his coffee break, before heading back to the HQ with the sergeant-major, both still in fits of laughter.

The two girls who worked in the offices were as amazed as everyone else that the colonel and the RSM were in such a jovial mood. By lunchtime the colonel called for the minibus and gave everyone the afternoon off and went home. Not needing an excuse the pathfinders opened up the bar.

The FAC course was held in Afrikaans and had to be continually translated into English for the foreigners. Major Grobelaar was a successful Impala pilot and instructed the class on the requirements of the air force when on joint operations with ground troops. The pathfinders, who only days before had been patrolling and fighting in Angola and some of whom were still sporting fresh wounds, found it difficult to adapt to a classroom environment. The major had a bit of a temper and would often start screaming and shouting in Afrikaans, much to their amusement which didn't help matters.

Lectures on landing zones and drop zones filled the days before the theory was put into practice and the men found themselves guiding in helicopters, first Alouettes then Pumas. This was followed by guiding Dakotas to parachute drop zones during the day and then at night. Much to the chagrin of the paras lined up at the door ready to jump, if the major wasn't happy with the talk-on he would suddenly stop the approach and tell them to do it again. As a result the plane would go round in another circle to repeat the whole process. He did this on several occasions, with the paras getting extremely fidgety. Later on in the pub there were a few heated discussions between the paras and the pathfinder students on the matter, but fortunately, even with the beer flowing, it never came to blows.

Finally, Impalas were directed onto targets for bombing and strafing runs. A couple of days before the course ended Colonel Breytenbach arrived to collect his men, saying that they had a lot of admin to sort out. A high level of activity at the air base had already been noticed by the men and it would seem that something was in the air.

The funeral of Steven Hadlow took place during this fortnight of training, and pathfinders not under instruction returned from the border to form the funeral party. Their brown uniforms were cleaned and pressed, having never previously worn the smarter 'stepout' order of dress that would have been the more appropriate uniform for such a formal parade.

As they became available, the men took flights back to Ondangwa where crews were assigned to Sabres and preparations made for vehicle operations. Throughout their time on the border the men were aware that they were the cause of some irritation to SWAPO, but the wish was for some large-scale decisive action that would do real damage to the terrorist organization. As each deployment came along, they would speculate whether this was 'the big one'. At that stage there was no suggestion that this one would be anything other than one of their standard operations. The colonel was present but he was giving nothing away.

Chapter 5
Operation Protea

Another 1.5-ton Unimog had been added to the Sabre convoy; this one had mounted a 60mm mortar in the back, so giving the company a greater indirect fire capability. In the open back of the vehicle was fitted a large truck tyre filled with sand soaked in diesel to give it a firm texture and support for the base plate. Gordon Brindley served as number one on the weapon, with his number two as CF para Steve Woodford, an old freefall parachuting colleague of Dave Barr's. Steve was doing a call-up in Sector 10 when he bumped into Dave, who introduced him to CSM Croukamp, a freefall parachutist himself. Steve was keen to get into action against SWAPO and asked if he could join the company on operations.

Throughout South Africa CF personnel were reporting as usual for their annual camps and boarding aircraft, expecting to be flown to various training areas. Instead, they found themselves landing at Grootfontein in South West Africa, where in total secrecy an invasion force was being gathered and formed into battle groups and task forces.

The Sabre convoy with all available pathfinders and a few South Africans up for a fight set off from Ondangwa at 0800 hours on 19 August, heading south to join the assembled force. A two-and-a-half-hour drive took them to the training area: bush land at Omuthiya near the town of Tsumeb. A vast amount of men and equipment was gathered and rehearsals had already reached an advanced stage. Upon arrival, the men were required to fill out medical and next-of-kin forms. As was standard practice for the pathfinders there was included a note requesting that next of kin be notified only in the event of death, but as had been the case previously the South Africans would ignore it and send out casualty notices anyway.

Hundreds of fighting vehicles filled the bush for miles around, including Ratel armoured infantry combat vehicles, Eland armoured cars, and more Buffels than the pathfinders thought possible. Self-propelled and drawn artillery completed the belligerent complement.

After days of comprehensive training and rehearsals the invading force lined up ready for the move to the FUP, the forming-up point, to cross into Angola.

Operation Protea was the culmination of months of secret planning. Unknown to the pathfinders, their earlier recce and fighting patrols were small but key elements in preparation for this invasion. They were ready to go in hard and inflict as much damage to SWAPO and FAPLA as they could; at last their long-held wishes were finally being fulfilled.

Colonel Breytenbach went to the operation headquarters to report his presence and ask for a job. The Pathfinder Company had not been included in the planning but the colonel was not going to let that prevent him from missing out on a good fight. He was tasked with tank-hunting as part of Battle Group 40. Tank-hunting with Land Rovers! No one could accuse the SADF of not trying out innovative ideas. The colonel returned to his men to give a general briefing.

Because of the massive build-up of conventional FAPLA forces in the southern towns of Angola, and the presence of Cuban troops and Warsaw Pact advisors, it was necessary to end permanently this threat to the border, and the support being afforded to SWAPO. Operation Protea was designed to smash the Soviet-supplied radar and air defences and neutralize the threat. The FAPLA armoured brigade at Xangongo 50 miles over the border was the first primary target to be attacked, and then the much fought-over town of Ongiva 95 miles to the east would be hit again. The destruction of SWAPO command structures, training and supply routes in the area would be achieved by hitting the several known base camps. After previous attacks these bases were now located in close proximity to FAPLA units in order to come under their protection. The physical layout of the bases had also changed; they'd

The Pathfinder Company was as keen as ever to take on SWAPO and their FAPLA allies; their role as tank-hunters caused not a moment's concern such was their confidence.

Top: A sense of tension could be detected from the columns of South African troops, many of whom had not seen action before, so Mark Griffiths and Gordon Brindley made oversized swords, axes and shields, which they used in light-hearted combat, battling each other between the vehicles. Temporarily at least spirits were lifted.

Above: The last vehicle to join the Sabre convoy was another 'Babymog', fitted to fire a 60mm mortar from the back. With it, Brindley was to engage and defeat a FAPLA machine gunner in one-on-one combat.

expanded in size over large undefined patches of the Angolan bush. Avoiding parade grounds and any solid buildings they'd now dug bunkers and trench systems deep into the ground which were well camouflaged to keep their presence hidden from prying South African eyes.

The next day the company began practising camp attacks with Task Force Alpha; they were issued French 89mm rocket launchers to replace their RPG-7s. Half a day was spent with familiarization and firing the heavier anti-tank weapons. Men of 32 Battalion made up a prominent part of the attack force and many old Rhodesian friends came over to the pathfinders' camp to renew old acquaintances. That night all those who had been recruited from outside South Africa gathered around a blazing fire and, with the help of a few beers and some lusty singing, celebrated the coming battle. Some of the more straight-laced South Africans could not understand this bonhomie and were heard to mutter, "Philistines!" and the pathfinders loved it.

On 21 August they were ordered to be ready to move any time after 1700 hours. The troops were assembled for a blessing by the dominee who focused totally on the fact that they were going to die and had better be prepared for the eventuality. Expecting a more inspirational sermon, the pathfinders were less than impressed with the performance. Peter Morpuss recalled the impression it left on him:

I could see on the faces of the National Service soldiers around me, who were youngsters, not much older than 18 or 19 and most probably had never seen combat before, that they were frightened. This was not the sort of thing they wanted to hear just before going on a major external raid.

The following day, at 1100 hours, the company was given its final briefing: Task Force Alpha would attack target Yankee, which was the town of Xangongo, and the FAPLA armoured brigade positioned there. As tank-hunters, the Pathfinder Company would remain uncommitted but ready to be deployed as required. By 1745 hours the task force was heading

Top left: Sergeant Bob Beech's Land Cruiser, driver Kiwi Watson, gunner Rich Malson with 'Irish' Mahon as his number 2.

Top right: The 14.5mm vehicle ready for action.

Above left: Australian and ex-Selous Scout, Sergeant Derrick Andrews commanded the 14.5mm Babymog.

Above right: Every deployment was affected by hold-ups caused by the vehicles getting bogged down in muddy vleis or soft sand. Here a tyre is changed; thorn punctures were a constant problem, but fortunately mechanical problems never occurred when the Sabres were in direct contact with the enemy.

Captain Peak's Land Cruiser.

to its form-up point (FUP), and by midday on 23 August it reached Okalongo, 30 kilometres from the cut line, where a major refuelling programme was carried out. The FUP was reached shortly afterwards.

The move from the FUP to the target started at 0230 hours the next morning. Crossing the cut line, a Unimog carrying a multiple rocket launcher detonated a mine and became the first casualty of Operation Protea. The Sabre convoy brought up the rear of this particular column of vehicles, eating dust and being bounced around on the rutted path cratered deeply by the passage of the heavy lorries ahead. So Colonel Breytenbach took the company on a parallel route by which he was able to avoid the stragglers and advance up the column.

Attack

At exactly noon two SAAF Mirages struck Xangongo. The ground forces, including the pathfinders, were already on the outskirts and watched the air strikes go in, along with the anti-aircraft response from FAPLA. The town's defences, under Soviet advice, were concentrated on the eastern, southern and western sides to prevent a massed frontal attack. But historically South Africa's military tactics had always demonstrated a preference for mobility and manoeuvre, so the attack came from the northeast.

At midday on 24 August bombing and strafing runs by Mirage jets announce the arrival of the South Africans at Xangongo. The Pathfinder Company did not form part of the assault force but moved into the town independently.

32 Battalion provided the assault troops who, supported by artillery fire from 155mm G5 guns, formed a sweep line and advanced on the town. An Eland armoured car knocked out a T-34 tank with its 90mm cannon, but most of the defenders' fire was from long-range weapons. The enemy withdrew from the area, leaving their tanks and other armoured fighting vehicles scattered in the streets and fields.

Word was passed down to the assaulting troops not to loot or otherwise investigate enemy equipment due to reported booby traps which had already killed friendly forces. As the town gradually came under South African control Colonel Breytenbach's command section proceeded to the 'Russian house', a property where the Soviet advisors had been living. They too were now running away as fast as they could. By this time the pathfinders were all wearing captured Soviet helmets in celebration of the day's events, but they were told to remove them owing to any confusion that might ensue. Their Sabres were the only camouflage-painted vehicles in the attack and were unfamiliar to many in the other SADF

As the aerial bombardment subsided, the pathfinder convoy entered the town from the north.

units. In fact they had earlier in the day come under distant fire from 32 Battalion who mistook them for the enemy. By 1900 hours the town was fully in South African hands. That night the Pathfinder Company took a position outside Fort Rocades, a Portuguese citadel situated in the centre of town on a high promontory overlooking the area, from where their machine guns could dominate any counter-attack from across the Cunene Bridge.

Tinned food donated to the terrorists from various charities in Sweden and Norway was found and made a very pleasant evening meal. Sentries were posted while the remainder bedded down under whatever cover they could find in case of mortar attack.

Late into the night a heavy contact nearby got the men stood to, but as it happened they weren't directly involved in the shootout which was caused by an enemy vehicle mounting three 14.5 machine guns appearing in the town centre. Gordon Brindley recalled the moment:

> My number two and I lay in a sunken rubbish pit near the barracks and as I lay back relaxing I remember seeing a stream of tracer fired up from the town ricocheting off the corner of a nearby building like a laser show. I looked over the town below and saw an RPG exploding in mid air; it was a very exciting show of fireworks.
>
> Then CSM Croukamp called us both onto the open parade square with our Pakmor mortar and a crate of bombs and told us to drop illumination rounds over the bridge since some FAPLA were trying to drive across and escape; this we duly did. Later I met an engineer who had witnessed our exercise and he told me that he thought that we were very brave since the whole area was alive with tracer rounds. I personally couldn't remember any tracer rounds but it would have been typical of Croukamp since he seemed to ignore such things.

The FAPLA soldiers apparently must have been hiding somewhere and mistakenly thought the South Africans had departed. Their mistake was corrected when they were all soon killed. The burned-out vehicle and their charred bodies were still blocking the road the next morning when a foot patrol was sent to check the company's perimeter.

Peter Morpuss was in that patrol:

> I heard an explosion and saw a soldier running towards us who said that someone had been wounded. Being a medic I ran back with him. The soldier was badly injured; he had shrapnel in his chest area and one arm had been blown off at the elbow. I gave him morphine straight away but had problems trying to get an IV drip into him, finally finding a vein by his ankle. Although I was talking to him the whole time and telling him he was going to be okay I could see that he was fading and within five minutes he died, I felt sorry for him being so young. His friend said the injuries were from a bobby trap; apparently a grenade pin was attached by wire to a door and was hidden under a blanket and other clothing, so that when the soldier opened the door the pin was pulled out. He then apparently went to pull the blanket away to see what was hidden under it when the grenade went off.

All was quiet by midday on the 25th. 61 Mechanized Brigade had arrived to take over in Xangongo, freeing 32 Battalion to go proceed to Ongiva and their next mission. Colonel Breytenbach again visited the operation headquarters and

Sergeant Andrews surveys the deserted streets of the town; fortunately the civilian population remained largely unaffected by the military operation.

Evidence of the air attack was everywhere. The initial resistance gave way to a general withdrawal, as FAPLA deserted Xangongo in chaotic fashion, abandoning their tanks and armoured cars. Some FAPLA units got detached in the confusion and it was these that had sporadic contact with South African forces through the afternoon and evening.

arranged for his men to be attached to Battle Group 30 who were tasked to head northwest and secure the open flank.

Joining up with Ratel infantry combat vehicles, the pathfinders made good progress along the tarmac road towards the town of Cahama to investigate a known FAPLA camp 55 miles to the northwest of Xangongo. They went through the motions of their attack drills but the camp was already deserted by the time the column reached it.

Leaving the main battle group the Pathfinder Company went off to investigate a nearby Catholic-run hospital. As the convoy approached many military-aged patients in dressing gowns appeared on the veranda and watched apprehensively as the Sabres cruised up and down the tended lawns. However, with more important work to do than searching for enemy wounded the vehicles returned to the job at hand.

Another site visited was that of a radio transmitter whose massive aerial tower was reputed to be the highest structure in Angola. It was used to send communist propaganda broadcasts into South West Africa, and some months previous a Recce Commando raid had failed to demolish it due to strong FAPLA defences. The colonel was keen to carry out the mission on behalf of his old unit, but on radioing his intention to headquarters he was told in a strongly worded reply not to destroy it under any circumstances.

While still driving in the bush the command Sabre was stopped by two figures emerging from cover whom the colonel recognized as two of his old Recce Commandos: 'Rocky' van Blerk and 'Kaffir' Smit. They asked for a lift back to friendly forces but jumping aboard a Sabre they found that they were going in the opposite direction.

At last light the battle group units dispersed for the night with one Ratel infantry company remaining and blocking the road to halt any FAPLA forces coming down from Cahama. The pathfinders laagered up a short distance off the road, half a mile or so down from the Ratels, and went into their night routine.

At 2200 hours Dave Barr was on guard when a massive convoy of petrol-driven trucks and armoured cars passed by, heading northeast. As all the friendly forces, apart from the pathfinders, had diesel engines Dave quickly woke the sleeping crews. By now the convoy had reached the Ratels blocking the road and a sharp engagement took place, with intense small-arms, machine-gun and cannon fire, lasting between five and ten minutes.

It was then followed by a silence, broken only by the sound of the FAPLA convoy now driving back the way they had come. By chance they stopped again, right next to the pathfinders who were now stood-to at the machine guns on their vehicles. On command from Colonel Breytenbach, CSM Croukamp's vehicle-mounted mortar fired a para-illumination round which was the signal for all the vehicles on the side nearest the road to open fire. Individuals from the far side of the laager crossed over and assisted with rocket launchers, bloopers and small arms.

Recovering from their initial shock, FAPLA returned fire. Their communist tracer was usually green but this time they were firing red tracer from their double-barrelled 23mm anti-aircraft machine guns. The pathfinders also provided a mixture of red and green tracer with Canadian Sean Wyatt belting out rounds from the captured 14.5 atop the Minimog. A ferocious amount of tracer and ball rounds ripped through the bush and streaked across the sky, with the pathfinder machine gunners pouring bursts of rounds at the enemy muzzle flashes, and the number twos keeping the guns reloaded with fresh belts of ammunition. Gordon Brindley was fighting his own personal dual at that time with an enemy machine gun:

> During the initial firefight I was dropping mortar rounds from the back of the Unimog with Mark throwing me up caseloads of live HE rounds. The gunner of a 23 mm parked on the road about 75 metres away was sweeping back and forth with his gun and all I could see was a red stream of tracer trying to find me and coming so close at one stage that I flinched away from the stream of rounds.

Gordon eventually won his dual when the enemy machine gun ceased firing. The nearby artillery unit added to the surreal scene by firing illumination shells which slowly arced across the night sky, bathing the scene in an eerie grey light. FAPLA suddenly stopped firing and all was quiet again. The pathfinders had suffered no casualties or damage, but engine noises and shouting coming from the far side of the road indicated that the enemy might now be setting up mortars. It was standard Soviet training to use mortar fire to cover a withdrawal; the pathfinders had had previous experience of this. A ten-man patrol under Captain Velthuizen was quickly formed and, armed with the anti-tank rocket launchers, they hurriedly made their way toward the sounds.

Top: The old Portuguese citadel Fort Rocades, where the pathfinders took position for the night, dominated the high ground and overlooked the Cunene River bridge.

Above and facing: Pathfinders Jim Burgess, Paul Whitehead and Sergeant Gillmore take in the ruins of the once-impressive citadel. The barrack accommodation gave up its loot to their need for FAPLA uniforms and equipment. However, extreme care was necessary because booby traps had already killed one South African, and more would fall victim before the operation was over.

The road was built up higher than the surrounding countryside so crossing it caused a tense moment as they were unavoidably exposed to view; but they got across safely, guided as they were by the excited voices of the enemy making no attempt at silence. Through the darkness and scrubby bush the enemy could be seen in busy preparation around some lorries. The pathfinders formed a firing line where each had a clear view of the targets not more than 15 yards away. Jim Burgess carried a rocket launcher and was positioned on the right of Captain Velthuizen who placed his hand on Jim's shoulder. When all was settled he gave a simple "OK"; Jim rose up on one knee and fired a rocket into the nearest lorry

This Soviet vehicle carrying three 14.5mm machine guns and crew attempted a breakout during the night but after a fierce firefight they were all killed and the vehicle burned out.

which exploded in a blinding flash. Another pathfinder fired a rocket into a second lorry as everyone opened up.

Enemy fire was initially returned before they could be seen running away. Dave Barr was firing 40mm grenades from his M79 blooper and seeing the enemy movement raised the trajectory to drop the grenades onto their line of flight. Recognizing the potential dangers of sweeping a live contact area in the dark, the patrol returned to the camp. After a quick reorganization it was apparent that the action was over for the night, so sentries were posted while the rest tried to catch up on some long-overdue sleep, but exploding ammunition in the burning vehicles made a din for some time to come.

The morning of 26 August found an air of excited expectation in the Pathfinder Company laager. They rose before dawn and after a brief stand-to had a quick breakfast and a mug of tea. The vehicles were loaded up and with the colonel's Sabre leading, they snaked through the bush and on to the road. To everyone's great satisfaction, the entire FAPLA convoy was found, deserted and almost intact on the road. It consisted of a fully equipped radio jeep, several BTR armoured personnel carriers, some BRDM armoured cars, four BM-21 multiple rocket launchers ('Stalin Organs') and four GAZ trucks, each with twin 23mm anti-aircraft machine guns mounted on the back. These captured vehicles, plus the two lorries already destroyed, made for a successful night's work. No enemy bodies were found which suggested that they had retreated with an element of control, taking their dead and wounded with them. There was much blood spoor and drag marks, which indicated that casualties had indeed been removed.

A search of the area did not produce much in the way of intelligence, but abandoned FAPLA webbing packs were all found to contain new uniforms. This unworn clothing, in FAPLA camouflage, had labels stitched inside declaring in English: 'Made in Cuba'. The Pathfinders gathered all these up for future use on clandestine operations.

Lacking any available men to drive the captured convoy, it was left to other South African forces to recover it and drive the vehicles back to South West Africa. With orders to return to Xangongo, the colonel had one last task to complete, for his own satisfaction, before heading back. The command Sabre drove to the radio transmitter mast visited the day before, and this time he ordered the crew to bring it down. Not having any time restraints the task was one that could be enjoyed, so Dave Barr, confident in the destructive power of his twin 50 calibres, emptied belts of ammunition at the base of the iron girder tower, but to no effect. Next Bruce Spanner and Paul Whitehead fired anti-tank rockets from the 89mm launchers which, more surprisingly, also had no effect. With playtime over Dave appeared with a large adjustable spanner and undid the securing bolts on two of the six steel-wire hawsers which supported the tower; it swayed, leaned over a bit, then slowly crumpled to the ground, causing the spectators to hastily withdraw: the highest structure in Angola no longer. Back at Xangongo, with no hero's welcome awaiting them, they were shunted out of the way to get cleaned up and work on their vehicles. Pete Morpuss's Land Rover was continually causing hold-ups due to breakdowns, which each repair failed to rectify. Several tyres also needed mending due to the never-ending puncture problem.

Writing later, Colonel Breytenbach recalled this moment:

> We sat around Xangongo for a day or two while somewhere up the line of command some senior officer
> contemplated what to do with these awkward pathfinders. We were not welcome in the lines of 61
> Mech and even less welcome in the top structure of Sector 10. My pathfinders were virtually banished
> to an 'isolation' area because there was a perception that they would contaminate 61 Mech with some
> strange, outlandish disease if they mixed with young National Servicemen.

The abandoned house given to the company as quarters became decorated with graffiti artwork of a particularly right-wing nature. Nothing offensive and not such a crime on the greater scale of things, but the South Africans were bringing news reporters into the town to witness the medical aid and food distribution being extended to the civilian population, so did not want the embarrassment the building would cause. The pathfinders learned that after they left the area a bulldozer was called in and knocked it down.

Eventually Colonel Breytenbach was given a new task: to head toward the town of Chivemba, a farther 80 miles north and the home base of the FAPLA force they had just ambushed on the road. Military intelligence indicated the presence of an extensive SWAPO base in the vicinity, and it was the colonel's job to find it and attack it. On the 27th at 0830 hours the Pathfinder Company, under command of Battle Group 10, left Xangongo at 1230 hours on their independent mission. Pete Morpuss's Sabre vehicle remained behind for repairs, much to the annoyance of the crew. The Angolan countryside here was quite different from that which the pathfinders were used to operating in. It was still thinly populated, but

Above and right: Tanks, armoured fighting vehicles, artillery, and all manner of military hardware were left abandoned for the South Africans to gather and take back to South West Africa.

Below right: 'Merc' Griffiths sporting one of the Soviet helmets much favoured by the men. Having already been shot at by 32 Battalion the previous day the pathfinders were warned not to wear them to avoid further confusion. The one-kilometre-long bridge over the Cunene River can be seen in the background. The Pathfinder Company crossed the river and joined the column of Battle Group 30 advancing to the northwest.

Top: The Cunene River Bridge.

Above: During the advance the crews fired into a SWAPO camp to the side of the road, but it proved to be deserted.

the terrain was more varied which did not allow the free vehicle movement they had become accustomed to. Rocks, hills, gullies and impenetrable bush made progress painfully slow and, often defeated by one route, they would have to retrace their tracks and make a new attempt elsewhere. By 1800 hours they had laagered up five kilometres south of Chivemba, which they believed contained a FAPLA force of unknown size.

Having deliberately made their presence known in the area, they lay in ambush along the road, hoping to catch any patrols foolhardy enough to come after them. Being deep in FAPLA territory it was a sound plan, but the enemy was not taking the bait and the night passed without incident. At 0600 hours the pathfinders had a quick breakfast but remained in ambush positions. After checking in on the high-frequency radio net to the controlling station, all was confirmed ready by 1100 hours to move off toward the SWAPO camp, the target of the mission.

Arriving in the area of the SWAPO camp at 1300 hours Sergeant Gillmore again threw up a sloping wire antenna to get comms with headquarters; Colonel Breytenbach, using his call sign 'Carpenter', requested helicopter gunship support for the attack. With the Alouettes on their approach the Sabres took up attack formation. The camp area was situated in open ground with good fields of fire for the defenders. Two Sabres were tasked to drive rapidly up one flank to engage any terrorists fleeing to the rear, while the remaining vehicles advanced fast in line on the camp, relying on surprise and firepower to give them the advantage.

The adrenalin kick heightened their senses and with eyes straining to pick up any sign of the enemy the pathfinders bounced over and through the scrubland until they found themselves in the centre of the bush complex ... alone. The camp had been empty for a number of days. There was no intelligence to be gathered, nor any sign of occupation. Disappointed by the outdated intelligence that had sent them on

The column neared Cahama but stopped for the night short of the town. Ratel infantry fighting vehicles from 61 Mechanized Brigade provided the infantry for the advance. Towed artillery supported the battle group.

Fortunately the explosives and ammunition in the vehicle had not added to the power of the initial detonation, but now, as the pathfinders watched, burning petrol set them off in another crashing explosion, which completely obliterated the vehicle.

Pathfinders survey the result of the previous night's fighting; the entire FAPLA convoy lies abandoned on the road. FAPLA were disciplined enough to retrieve their dead and wounded during their retreat.

Surprise gave the Pathfinder Company an initial advantage during the nighttime fighting. But FAPLA, who were equally heavily armed, disengaged when the volume and accuracy of the pathfinders' fire proved more effective.

this fool's errand; they could now add yet another 'lemon' to their list of failed missions. But all was not lost; they had advanced much farther into enemy territory in the hunt for SWAPO or FAPLA, much farther that headquarters had ever wanted. For the rest of the day a number of possible sites were visited, each time the men tense in anticipation of immediate action, but each time neither sight nor sound of the enemy was detected; except that is for indiscriminately planted landmines.

On a number of occasions crewmen spotted partially uncovered mines lying visible in the ground. To their unprotected vehicles this was a serious threat, so their movement north was undertaken with great difficulty by avoiding the dirt roads.

Next day, the 29th, it was decided to enter Chivemba itself. As one of the Land Rovers had broken down, Colonel Breytenbach left the mechanics to sort it out, protected by a section of two vehicles, while he approached the town with the remaining seven vehicles and a total of 26 men.

Top: The advance into the town of Chivemba was halted when the command Sabre hit an anti-tank mine.

Above: Colonel Breytenbach and Lang Price were shaken by the experience but continued soldiering. Sergeant Gillmore and Dave Barr were uplifted by casevac helicopter.

In the kraals on the edge of town Captain Velthuizen's two Sabres led the advance to contact. They then turned left through a gap in the fence to an open field, followed some distance behind by the colonel's Land Cruiser. A deafening explosion and a cloud of black smoke and dust suddenly enveloped the command Sabre, which immediately burst into a fiery inferno.

In the front of the vehicle the colonel and driver, Lang Price, were remarkably still in their seats until they stumbled out, stunned, with the colonel bleeding from shrapnel wounds (the third time he had been blown up). In the back Sergeant Gillmore was violently thrown out, landing about 15 yards away with collarbone broken and one foot dangling free from the shattered ankle; he was conscious but confused. Dave Barr was tossed high into the sky, landing back into the blazing wreck, and with both legs broken and bent at acute angles he was unable to help himself as the conflagration engulfed him. Colonel Breytenbach at once leaped aboard the flaming vehicle to manhandle Barr free, then, with Lang's assistance, carried the wounded soldier a safe distance from the blaze.

The remaining Sabres formed a defensive perimeter as Australian Sergeant Derek Andrews collected up Gillmore and carried him to a safer position on one of the unharmed Sabres. It was not clear what caused the explosion; had they been under attack? But as no further enemy action took place it was realized that it must have been a boosted anti-tank mine which the left-rear wheel of the command vehicle had detonated. Fortunately the explosives and ammunition in the vehicle had not added to the power of the initial detonation, but now, as the pathfinders watched, burning petrol set them off in another crashing explosion, which completely obliterated the vehicle.

Colonel Breytenbach's priority was to get the wounded evacuated. With the seriousness of their condition a three-day drive south was not an option. The morphine substitute Sosegon had been administered to the two critical casualties but as the effects of shock wore off the open wounds began to bleed freely. The wounded were put on Rob Gilmour's Unimog and the convoy withdrew a safe distance back down the path they had come up.

HF radio communication back to 61 Mechanized headquarters at Xangongo was established before the colonel requested helicopter casevac; but he was angered when the commander told him directly that unarmed helicopters were not authorized to fly so far north into enemy territory. Attempts at reason were ignored and the official decision stood: no casevac. However, one fearless, or compassionate, Alouette helicopter pilot did respond and radioed to say he would come and rescue the casualties. This he did despite the brigade commander yet again refusing him permission to do so, but the pilot ignored him and confirmed he was on his way.

Thirty minutes later one of the pathfinders threw yellow smoke to guide the Alouette helicopter onto their position, as the pilot, later identified as Hojan Cronjé (a brave man ideed), landed and loaded up the wounded, who were taken directly to the aid station at Xangongo and then on to the military hospital at Oshakati. The colonel and Lang, now without any weapons or equipment, took up a new position on one of the stores' Unimogs.

The helicopter pilot reported strong enemy forces in the town, so there was nothing for the Pathfinder Company to do except make their way back to friendly lines. Off-road going was still difficult but their spirits did pick up after a minor brush with SWAPO, which occurred later in the day when the leading vehicle emerged from thick bush right next to a group of resting terrorists. Taking the only course of action possible, it charged straight into them shooting from all sides, and in a moment all the terrorists were dead, either shot or run over.

Revenge for the loss of the Sabre came quickly when this SWAPO gang was surprised and wiped out.

At Ondangwa captured equipment was displayed for publicity purposes and inventory-taking. With so much captured weaponry recovered, the novelty soon wore off.

On searching the bodies it was found that one was a woman, a Zambian ex-teacher. But more importantly this little contact provided weapons and blankets for the colonel and Lang.

Arriving back at Xangongo, the company found that the South African forces were packing up to return south. Driving first to Ongiva which was taken by the South Africans after a three-day fight, then over the cut line into South West Africa, they finally arrived at Ondangwa during the afternoon of 1 September. The men and vehicles were exhausted, but not so much that they couldn't hold a party that evening for CSM Croukamp, Lang Price and Rob Gilmour who would be returning to Murrayhill having completed their one-year engagements.

Chapter 6
Post-Protea operations

Back to Murrayhill

The pathfinders would have been delighted to turn round and redeploy operationally straight away but instead there followed a period of frustration at remaining unused in camp. Colonel Breytenbach reported to Brigadier Badenhorst at Sector 10 Headquarters, and was again left in no doubt that he and the pathfinders were not welcome in the sector.

The colonel himself came in for specific attention. The very desirable Soviet jeep captured in the FAPLA road ambush had found its way into the pathfinders' hands and Colonel Breytenbach had every intention of keeping it for his own use now that his Sabre was no more. The brigadier ordered the colonel to hand it over to the Military Police who were dealing with all the captured equipment, but the colonel found a broken-down vehicle which he surrendered to the MPs instead. The good vehicle was then given to the Recce Commandos for their pseudo operations.

Once the post-operational maintenance and repairs had been carried out, the pathfinders found themselves redundant in camp, where fairly pointless menial tasks were demanded of them, simply to stop them idling away the days. Each evening they braaied their food as they were still not allowed to

Being left idle at Ondangwa in the summer heat was not conducive to the men's well-being; they naturally reverted to drinking.

Back at Murrayhill and being the veteran soldiers they were, the pathfinders could turn out as smart as any other when the occasion required it.

eat in the main mess hall; beer provided their relaxation and entertainment. An attempt was made by Captain Peak to introduce a two-can-per-night limit in order to contain the drunkenness, but none of the men thought it could be a serious request so tended to ignore the instruction.

There developed a never-ending card school. Jim Burgess, KD Clark and Ken Gaudet were the nucleus, usually attracting about six or seven players. They played poker for considerable stakes as Scotsman Jim took satisfaction in beating the Americans at their own game. Drinking levels increased because they were getting all the free beer they wanted from the air force base personnel in exchange for bits of kit they had looted during Operation Protea. A FAPLA shirt was worth a case; extra if there was blood on it, so they killed a chicken and smeared blood on the enemy uniforms. Communist bayonets were what the air force people really wanted and the men were happily able to oblige.

For nearly three weeks the company endured this boredom, with each day getting hotter and the mosquitoes more aggressive as summer developed. Then on 18 September they were told to pack their kit and be ready to fly back to Pretoria early the next morning. This they did but it all happened so fast, without following the usual 'clearing-out' procedure, that they thought it highly suspicious.

On landing at Waterkloof air force base near Pretoria they met new pathfinder selection candidates waiting to board the same plane to be taken up to the Caprivi Strip. One of the instructors travelling with them was Carl Saltzman, his

Above and previous two pictures: Familiarization with mine-laying and other military skills, to assist in the retraining of the CF paras, kept the men occupied after Operation Protea.

damaged eye now permanently sightless. Of the other previously wounded pathfinders, Rich Malson was still in hospital awaiting treatment for his eye injury, while Sergeant Graham Gillmore's shattered ankle was being rebuilt with bone grafts. Dave Barr's leg joints were not mending and despite his valiant efforts to overcome the pain there was no improvement. One leg was amputated below the knee, and then shortly afterwards the same leg was amputated above the knee, and then, finally after weeks of dashed hopes, the other leg had to be removed from below the knee.

Following a couple of days in camp at Murrayhill the company was given leave for a week. The colonel explained to them that their hurried return from the border was the result of a misunderstood telephone message. But the men were happy to be on leave with healthy savings in the bank and were not going to fret over it; they were going to hit the town.

By the following week the men were broke and hopeful of returning to Ondangwa. They were told that the flight would only be in a week's time, so had to pass the time with little to do. However, evenings were spent letting their hair down in Pretoria and staying one step ahead of the authorities. A social evening organized by the American Embassy was disrupted by Jim Burgess snatching down an Irish flag, it being a symbol of the hated IRA. As the day of departure loomed they were then informed that they would not be going for yet another week, so without money they were obliged to let their hair down in camp which meant that it was more difficult to stay out of trouble.

WOII McAleese was appointed acting CSM of the Pathfinder Company and began a training programme in camp. Mine-laying techniques, map reading, house clearing and bunker clearing were covered under his supervision. The instruction then continued with the pathfinders themselves assisting in the retraining of a large number of CF paratroopers recently called up by 2 and 3 Parabat.

On 22 October it was announced that those pathfinders who had been previously parachute trained but did not have their South African qualification would be doing a conversion course. Initial fears that it would involve the Bloemfontein Parachute School run-around were quashed when they were told it would only entail them doing one jump the next day. However, ground training commenced under the guidance of the sergeant-major. A lorry took the men to the SAAF airfield at Waterkloof where after a bit of a wait but no further complications, they boarded the aircraft for a jump from 800 feet, although the men swore later that it was actually only 500 feet. The reason given for this sudden development was that a large-scale exercise was beginning the next day and that the pathfinders were needed to take part along with the Parabats.

On returning to Murrayhill they paraded and were presented with their new para wings from Colonel Fraser, the Commanding Officer of 3 Parabat. However, the men had no doubt that this exercise would soon turn out to be an operational airborne deployment.

Those previously para-trained pathfinders who did not have their South African wings were taken on one para drop to demonstrate their training. They were told it was for a forthcoming exercise but many suspected that an operation was in the air. Parading at Murrayhill they were presented with their wings and para beret badge by Colonel Fraser, Commanding Officer of 3 Parabat.

Pathfinders receive their wings.

Operation Daisy

The South Africans reviewed their achievements earned during Operation Protea. They had inflicted a thousand casualties on the enemy for the loss of ten men killed. Russian advisers and their wives were among the enemy dead, and one Warrant Officer Nicolai Pestretsov was captured. Several thousand tons of military hardware were seized, including tanks and other armoured vehicles: 250 vehicles in total. Many, many lorryloads of heavy machine guns, small arms, anti-tank and anti-aircraft weapons with ammunition and ancillary equipment were also captured or destroyed.

The smashing of SWAPO's infrastructure in the south of the country set their revolutionary plans back a year. But there was some criticism within the SADF that the attack on Ongiva would have brought even heavier SWAPO casualties if an airborne force had been deployed in the rear of the town to engage the fleeing terrorists. As it was the terrorists had been able to exit their positions and escape by melting into the bush.

On 24 October Captain Peak, CSM McAleese and the pathfinders, together with the CF Parabats, proceeded to Waterkloof air base and from there were flown to an undisclosed destination, which to no one's surprise turned out to be Grootfontein in South West Africa. They moved to a base camp and for the next six days got acclimatized to the extreme summer heat. Preparations for operations were made, weapons checked and the sights zeroed. Firing drills on the support weapons were brushed up and further tactical training instruction was given to the CF personnel.

Army Intelligence staff then gave the men a complete briefing of the task at hand. After the conclusion of Operation Protea, the SWAPO regional headquarters at Chitequeta, located in southeastern Angola 45 miles from the cut line, were attempting to regroup their scattered members. As a result Operation Daisy, as it was now officially called, would be an attack on the sprawling thirty-five-square-kilometres complex. 61 Mechanized Brigade would drive up to carry out the assault after an initial air attack by Canberra bomber aircraft dropping their 1,000-pound bombs. The paratroopers would be dropped behind the enemy lines from C-130 transport planes in the early hours before dawn, and move into likely positions to cut off enemy escape routes. Up to 2,000 terrorists were expected to be in the camp.

The airborne forces wait at Grootfontein for deployment into Angola for Operation Daisy.

The marking out of the drop zone would be carried out by Recce Commandos. This irked some of the pathfinders who had been trained for this specific task. They now found themselves divided up between the para companies in a 'roll-up' role. Once on the ground each attached group of pathfinders would collect, organize and guide the scattered paratroopers to their predetermined assembly points. Having formed such a close-knit unit the pathfinders would have preferred to deploy as a single force, but it was not to be.

While the focus during the day was on combat the usual evening routine of braai and beers was maintained. The men even had a lay-in on the 31st. The free time allocated was to allow them to pack and make final preparations for deployment. In the afternoon they practised their positions in the aircraft, and the re-organization of the rendezvous points on the DZ. An evening 'dry' rehearsal in the bush completed the day's activities.

A full dress rehearsal was carried out the next day, involving a drive to Grootfontein air base for a nighttime parachute drop from C-130 aircraft, and then a walk of about two kilometres through thick bush to the strobe light which indicated the RV. Several injuries occurred among the ranks of the CF paras as a result of this exercise, which unfortunately should have been expected as the result of a night jump onto a strange, unprepared DZ.

Various differences in operational attitudes between the foreigners and the South Africans quickly became apparent. The battle orders passed down to the men were only for a two-day deployment, so as a result the CF paras were only lightly loaded with water and rations. By contrast the pathfinders, having experienced intelligence briefings before, took rations for a week, a full load of spare ammunition, and a higher-than-usual amount of extra weaponry. Gordon Brindley was attached to A Company, 3 Parabat and was ridiculed by the paras when he struggled with his heavy-framed rucksack containing all his kit, including spare radio batteries. His rifle and M79 blooper with extra bandoliers of grenades also did not go without comment when an officer threatened to have him charged over his R4 rifle ammunition consisting only of tracer rounds with the heads cut down. The comment was of course treated by Brindley with the contempt it deserved.

On 3 November the time to deploy for real finally arrived; at midmorning lorries took the airborne forces to Grootfontein where they had a pitiful excuse for a hot meal. At this moment of high anticipation the pathfinders were hit with some shattering news: the company was going to be disbanded in December and the men were to be transferred to 32 Battalion. Mixed feelings filled the men's thoughts: would it be a good thing to be up where the fighting was or would they be better off staying as pathfinders? Not that they had a choice at that stage. Other news to reach them was more immediate: ground forces in Angola had already engaged the enemy. The action had started and they were only hours away from an operational parachute descent.

At 0100 hours in the morning of the 4th the troops kitted up and boarded six C-130s for the three-hour flight to the DZ. The heat was oppressive and the humidity stifling. Gordon Brindley's experience though was not typical:

The lads were well behaved in the plane with no grumbling or anyone being airsick. We got the order to 'stand up, hook up' which was repeated by all the paratroopers in unison. I was the last man on the starboard side; we then did our equipment checks and told off from the rear of the stick. The order 'action stations' was given and we stamped to the open door. The order to 'stand in the door' must have been given but I didn't hear anything.

The green light went on and the stick started to jump out of the door. I felt as though nothing was happening as the men in front of me concertinaed as if in a traffic jam. All of a sudden the plane started lurching from air turbulence and I saw Captain Peak move very quickly down the now almost-empty plane. Suddenly the pull was gone and I ran down the empty plane with such force that I overshot the door and ended up in the arms of the dispatcher but I then pushed so hard away from his grasp that I flew out of the door backwards into the black void.

I still can't understand to this day how the static line didn't remove my head. A split second later I was in a different world of absolute quiet and darkness. It was as if I had wakened from a nightmare. I automatically went through the in-flight drills of checking that my canopy was deployed, which was a waste of time since I couldn't even see my hand in front of my face. Then I carefully ran my hands down my harness until I found the release lever for the rucksack. I did the same with the other hand and after tucking my feet behind me released both levers simultaneously. I waited for the tug on my harness to signify that the rucksack was

Jim Burgess safely on the ground.

146

Gordon Brindley also drained by the heat but carrying sufficient water.

under me and still attached when I heard the heart-rending sound of it crashing through trees; despite what the briefing major had said about flat ground, we were landing in trees. I quickly crossed my arms and squeezed my legs together and crashed straight through a tree and waited for the impact of the ground. Nothing happened! I sensed that I was bouncing around in my harness above the ground, but how high? Being stuck in a tree in enemy territory is every parachutist's nightmare. Most of the old lads carried a knife in their webbing; I drew mine and cut the rigging lines of the parachute intending to drop to the ground, when unexpectedly I felt terra firma and realized that I was only about six inches in the air.

Because of the disrupted dispatch from the aircraft the squad of pathfinders attached to A Company landed in close proximity to one another but away from the main body of paratroopers. Since the 'roll-up' drill on the DZ involved gathering the scattered paratroops and bringing them back to the pathfinder's location, Captain Peak decided that it was unnecessary to carry all the heavy rucksacks while performing the task. So he and the Frenchman Gilbert left their heavy equipment with the other four pathfinders of the group, which included Rhodesian Sergeant Penrose, ex-Foreign

Jim Burgess, KD Clark, Peter Morpuss and Mac McEwan are drained by the heat and lack of water.

Legionnaire Sergeant Ozzie Overall, Gordon Brindley and Rhodesian Bruce Spanner. Using the location as a fixed RV location the two went off to gather up the Parabat Company. However, once they disappeared into the darkness, those remaining pathfinders in the group did not see their colleagues again, nor anybody else for two days. The aircraft approach had been from a direction totally different from what had been initially planned, and as a result the original information that the RV was on the same alignment as they had parachuted in on was now wrong. Meanwhile Captain Peak did manage to gather the company together and headed off to the correct tactical location, but the four pathfinders were left behind as a consequence.

Over at C Company the pathfinder squad there consisted of CSM McAleese, Jim Burgess, Peter Morpuss, KD Clark, Mac McEwan and Sean Wyatt, who also had a story to tell. Their aircraft approach was off line so the pilot took them round again, only for that attempt to be aborted as well. He finally got the green light for the jump on his third run-in. By this time the paratroopers had been stood to the door for thirty minutes in stifling heat and buckling under the weight of their rucksacks. They still ended up ten kilometres from their intended target, but the pathfinders regrouped the company and led them on the route to their correct position. By this time the sun was up and they were grateful of the shade offered by the trees. Each company moved to its area of operations where it was to locate and engage any SWAPO it found. C Company moved into position to ambush a road that Military Intelligence said was used regularly; it looked to them to be anything but.

Two days came and went, the CF paratroopers were out of rations and everybody was out of water, intense heat sucked the moisture out of their bodies, leaving everyone severely dehydrated. Some patrolling was necessary but mostly they kept to the shade, yet ten men still needed intravenous saline drips to stop them from becoming severely ill. A hole was dug in the dried-up water course of the Bambi River and some water was found. Despite the fact that it was a murky grey colour, due to the recent bush fires, the water was a welcome addition to the sparse supply available. By this time all the drips carried by the men had

Top: A SWAPO killed by Sean Wyatt.

Above: Jim Burgess and Mac McEwan with dead SWAPO.

been opened and drunk when, on the third day, some water was brought out to them by helicopter. A previous air supply, using an air-dropped rubber container, had proved a failure when on contact with the ground the container burst.

The companies moved position in their hunt for SWAPO. FAPLA ground forces stayed right out of contact during this operation; however, the Angolan Air Force did get involved until a SAAF Mirage shot down a MiG-21.

On one movement of the company, guided by CSM McAleese, he spotted a group of SWAPO up ahead. The patrol had every advantage of surprise, so the CSM silently set about arranging the men for assault. In the lead were the CSM and his pathfinders, with a platoon of paratroopers spread out behind them, but as they began their advance on the enemy position a CF paratrooper accidentally fired his rifle. With surprise lost a firefight began, with Sean Wyatt hitting a terrorist with a grenade round from the M79. The SWAPO terrorists quickly ran off, leaving the company to sweep the contact area. The one dead terrorist turned out to be the second-in-command for logistics and had a wealth of useful information, carried in his leather pouch.

The airborne troops subsequently had a number of running skirmishes with SWAPO but nothing decisive and certainly not the high number of kills that was originally envisaged. The four pathfinders initially abandoned by A Company had dug in in a small defensive position, awaiting a possible assault by hundreds of fleeing terrorists. In the meantime they had not wasted the opportunity of looting the contents of the packs of their absent friends and now had surplus food and water. Eventually hearing aircraft noise they fired a flare and were spotted by a helicopter which was searching for them. On a lighter note, the situation was made confusing when it was announced that the aircarft was looking for "a Brindley and Penrose with an overall and a spanner". The pilot of the helicopter threw down a message written on a crumpled piece of paper to the four *uitlanders*, but written in Afrikaans it was unintelligible to them. The four set off in the direction of the helicopter where they soon met a patrol sent out to get them. They then continued the operation attached to D Company.

Finally, on 13 November all the para companies withdrew to a rear echelon area at an improvised bush airstrip. Here a solitary

Top: 'Irish' Mahon on the last pathfinder operation. By now the company was fully equipped with FAPLA uniforms and Soviet weaponry. Above: Jim Burgess.

Above left: The vehicle patrols entered many of the abandoned SWAPO camps that covered the area of operations. They were well constructed and would have been difficult to overcome.

Above right: Landmines again inflicted casualties. This stores' Unimog was repaired after a breakdown only to promptly hit a mine. When the engineers arrived to recover the vehicle they found 14 other Soviet TM56 anti-tank mines laid on the road.

Dakota ferried them back to Ondangwa in relays. Once back in their old camp the pathfinders compared individual war stories over a braai and several beers. Because of the lack of a positive result the men called the operation 'Op Flop'; they were less than impressed with the forces they had just worked with. For instance, when Gordon Brindley arrived at the D Company position he saw the desperate condition the paras were in due to their lack of water. Remembering their earlier laughter at the weight of his rucksack he was not tempted to offer any of them the clean, fresh water contained within it.

On other occasions the pathfinders would return from patrol to base to find sentries not at their post, and the men either in their underpants or sunbathing naked. The final straw for the pathfinders was the one and only time when they had the enemy at their mercy and a CF paratrooper had accidentally discharged his rifle, giving away their advantage.

However, Operation Daisy was considered a success by the SADF. Seventy-five enemy were killed during the deployment, another command and logistics base was destroyed and SWAPO were finally driven out of southern Angola. Another large haul of arms and ammunition recovered was an added bonus. So complete was South African control of this newly created buffer zone that they continued to use the airfield at Ongiva as a forward logistics base until the end of the conflict.

Looking to the future the pathfinders discovered that Colonel Breytenbach had been moved to a new job, training UNITA in the Caprivi Strip, and that the new commander at 44 Parachute Brigade was Colonel Frank Bestbier. One of his first decisions was to get rid of the troublesome Pathfinder Company for whom he had no need. The men were fully aware that they had been formed entirely at the whim of Colonel Breytenbach, and if the new commander would not use their skills then a future move to 32 Battalion's Reconnaissance Platoon was probably the best thing.

At Ondangwa on 14 November the company commenced the usual clean-up and preparation of their weapons, vehicles and personal kit, should they be called to action again. Then, only two days later they were given a warning order to be ready to deploy with the Sabre convoy under command of, and in support of, a 32 Battalion operation.

The original pathfinders were by now ending their one-year contracts and most had decided to explore pastures new, and their places in the vehicle crews were taken by the later arrivals. Captain Velthuizen and the CSM returned to Pretoria, leaving command of the company to Captain Peak who briefed the men on their latest deployment to be known as Operation Handbag. The company had been assigned the area between Xangongo and Ongiva to patrol. The enemy had been driven from the region during Operation Protea but it was necessary for SADF forces to maintain a presence to prevent any attempt by SWAPO to re-establish itself. Also, the pathfinders were instructed to engage any gangs crossing the area trying to infiltrate into South West Africa.

The Sabre convoy moved from Ondangwa to Okolongo on 19 November where they stopped for a couple of hours and changed from their brown uniforms into the FAPLA kit they had recently acquired. On crossing into Angola they headed north and had not been patrolling long when Sergeant Bob Beech narrowly missed a group of 15 SWAPO at a watering hole, so it was apparent that the enemy were present and that they might have some fighting on their hands. The next day they stayed in the town of Cuamato where the pathfinders had begun their active service almost a year before.

Captain Peak and the men took the opportunity to inspect the various old base camps set up by SWAPO, now lying abandoned. Some of these were extensive affairs with properly reinforced bunkers and sophisticated trench systems. One of the stores' Unimogs then broke an axle. The spare parts had to be sent out from base and caused the company to remain in the one area for a couple of days, not something they liked doing because it was inviting attack. Fortunately nothing happened, but on the third day, the 23rd, with the Unimog now repaired they moved off, only for the same

Gordon Brindley inspects the damage without realizing his foot is inches away from another landmine.

Lance-Corporal Jeb do Nascimento suffered a leg injury as a result of the explosion; he and Corporal Roy Meyer were casevaced by Puma helicopter.

vehicle to hit a landmine. The crew were thrown out, the driver Jeb do Nascimento and commander Roy Meyer were injured and required casevac, but crewman Fred Derret was only shaken up. As aid was being administered to the wounded men, vehicles could be heard approaching so the company immediately prepared for action, taking up positions to hit whomever came up the road. The tension was diffused when they saw that it was brown SADF Buffels carrying a company of 32 Battalion.

Alarmingly a second mine was spotted under the damaged Unimog and the pathfinders waited another day in the area for engineers to be brought in to defuse the mine and recover the vehicle. While engaged in this task, the engineers found another 14 Soviet TM56 mines laid in pairs in the immediate area. Once the vehicle recovery had been completed the convoy moved to a Lutheran Church mission at Shangalala, about ten kilometres from Xangongo, and here the medic Peter Morpuss gave aid to several local Africans who needed attention.

Another day was spent patrolling the general area and other abandoned SWAPO camps before they were ordered to return to Ondangwa, where they arrived on the 26th to be greeted by the CSM and the latest pathfinder selection course. Captain Peak reported to Sector 10 headquarters at Oshakati for debriefing after the patrol, but he may not have been prepared for the tirade he received from Brigadier Badenhorst who made it crystal clear yet again that the foreigners were not wanted in his sector, and that he was making arrangement for them to be removed.

In order to maintain morale and the combat readiness of the men CSM McAleese commenced a programme of retraining involving the new and old pathfinders. But it was a doomed attempt, and on 1 December a Sammel truck arrived to collect the company and take them on the five-hour drive to Grootfontein for a flight back to Pretoria. Once settled back at Murrayhill they immediately got involved in the training of more CF paratroopers from 3 Parabat, followed by a final exercise which involved a parachute drop near the radar station north of Murrayhill. SAAF security personnel with dog handlers then tried, and failed, to track them down.

Disbandment

On 15 December a number of men returned to Ondangwa to drive the Sabre convoy back, and then in January 1982 the Pathfinder Company was disbanded. On 18 February the men travelled to South West Africa for the last time, to be absorbed into 32 Battalion. A 44 Para Training Team was formed by Sergeant-Major Peter McAleese with Australian Corporal Terry Tangney and New Zealand Corporal Chris Rogers, both heavy combat veterans from Support Commando RLI, and Australian Sergeant Derek Andrews who was ex-Selous Scouts. The team's focus was to continue the successful work previously done in the retraining of the Citizen Force members and to accompany them on operations.

The ex-pathfinders did not settle at 32 Battalion which had its own distinctive method of operations and whose common language was Portuguese. The men were not wanted or needed by this specialist unit, so as their enlistments ran out they faded away. A sad end to a unit of such highly experienced combat soldiers.

Some remained in South Africa to lead civilian lives. Others returned to their homelands and re-enlisted in their own armed forces to pursue yet another chapter in their military careers. In London the VIP close-protection industry received a boost from several of the returning veterans, while others faded entirely from public view.

With his two artificial legs Dave Barr returned to freefall parachuting and his passion for Harley Davidson motorcycles. Riding solo around the world he created new Guinness world records and raised money for invalid charities, and through his motivational talks he has inspired many to overcome adversity.

Major MacKenzie continued a successful soldiering career in the Sultanate of Oman, Great Britain and New Zealand, retiring as a lieutenant-colonel. Pete McAleese was invited to lead a series of mercenary operations in Columbia, taking several ex-pathfinders with him.

Whatever the future held, and holds, for the veterans of the Pathfinder Company their shared experiences and comradeship remains a cherished bond between them. The Philistines revelled in their notoriety but it was for their self-motivation and fighting spirit that they want best to be remembered.

Pathfinder Company, 1 February 1982

Back row from left: L/Cpl B. Spanner, L/Cpl A. Hunter, L/Cpl B. Sonne, L/Cpl C. Horn, L/Cpl A. Mahon, L/Cpl C. Derret, L/Cpl K. Swanepoel, L/Cpl G.C. Watson, L/Cpl P. Macrae, L/Cpl M. Rousseau.

Third row: Cpl C. Saltzman, Cpl E. Debay, Cpl G. Evert, Cpl J. Burgess, Cpl N. Arnold, Cpl N. Fishbach, Cpl C. Rogers, L/Cpl M. Lowe.

Second row: Sgt P. Polzin, Sgt K.D. Clark, Sgt J. Wessels, Capt C.W.G. Peak, Lt F.T. Verduin, WOII P. McAleese, Sgt R.T. Beech, Sgt D.W. Andrews.

Front: Cpl T. Tangney, L/Cpl S.P. Turner, Cpl K. Crook, L/Cpl I. Dalglish, Cpl D. Borland.

Appendix

After a day of intense fighting, the attack on the SWAPO camp north of the Angolan town of Cuamato faltered and the South Africans withdrew from contact. The next morning, after SAAF aircraft and helicopter gunships softened up the camp, the paratroopers again advanced to the enemy's prepared positions. Pathfinders under CSM Peter McAleese again spearheaded the attack, with veteran war reporter Al J. Venter accompanying them. His article and photographs appeared in the South African magazine *Scope* a couple of months later. These pictures portray the action just as it happened in front of him, with lead still flying all around. Despite FAPLA assistance to SWAPO the camp fell to the parachutists after a morning of determined fighting.

All pictures from *Scope* magazine, March 1981.

Index